Think *Before* You Engage

Think *Before* You Engage

100 QUESTIONS TO ASK BEFORE STARTING A SOCIAL MEDIA MARKETING CAMPAIGN

Dave Peck

WILEY

John Wiley & Sons, Inc.

Think Before You Engage 100 Questions to Ask Before Starting a Social Media Marketing Campaign

Published by
John Wiley & Sons, Inc.
10475 Crosspoint Boulevard
Indianapolis, IN 46256
www.wiley.com

Copyright © 2011 by Dave Peck

Published simultaneously in Canada

ISBN: 978-1-118-01881-1

978-1-118-14736-8 (ebk)

978-1-118-14735-1 (ebk)

978-1-118-14734-4 (ebk)

Manufactured in the United States of America

10 9 8 7 6 5 4 3 2 1

For general information on our other products and services please contact our Customer Care Department within the United States at (877) 762-2974, outside the United States at (317) 572-3993 or fax (317) 572-4002.

Wiley also publishes its books in a variety of electronic formats. Some content that appears in print may not be available in electronic books.

Library of Congress Control Number: 2011930317

I would like to dedicate this book to my loving and supportive family—my wife, Jenn, our children, Xander, Brendan, Colby, Caroline, and Carter and let this remind them that "It is never too late to become what you might have been" (George Eliot).

About the Author

Dave Peck has been active in social media since 2004 and has been profiled on such networks as NBC, CNBC, and Current TV. His focus on viral, word of mouth (WOM) marketing and networking has allowed him to grow online communities for organizations such as Coca Cola, Harvard, UC Berkeley, and Wells Fargo. As a social media strategist, Dave has consulted and developed programs for *The Grammys, The Ozzy Osbourne Auction*, George Lynch, Stella McCartney, Sergio Rossi, Lee Meriwether, Antonio Sabato Jr., NPR, and many others. You can find Dave online at www.thedavepeck.com and on Twitter as @davepeck.

About the Technical Editor

Barry Moltz is an author and consultant who gets business owners growing again by unlocking their long-forgotten potential. With decades of entrepreneurial experience in his own business ventures as well as consulting for countless other entrepreneurs, Barry has discovered the formula to get stuck business owners out of their funk and marching forward. Barry applies simple, strategic steps to facilitate change for entrepreneurs, and gets them growing their business once again.

Credits

ACQUISITIONS EDITOR
Mary James

PROJECT EDITOR
Ginny Munroe

TECHNICAL EDITOR
Barry Moltz

SENIOR PRODUCTION EDITOR
Debra Banninger

COPY EDITOR
Apostrophe Editing Services

EDITORIAL MANAGER
Mary Beth Wakefield

FREELANCE EDITORIAL MANAGER
Rosemarie Graham

ASSOCIATE DIRECTOR
OF MARKETING
David Mayhew

MARKETING MANAGER
Ashley Zurcher

BUSINESS MANAGER
Amy Knies

PRODUCTION MANAGER
Tim Tate

VICE PRESIDENT AND EXECUTIVE
GROUP PUBLISHER
Richard Swadley

VICE PRESIDENT AND EXECUTIVE
PUBLISHER
Neil Edde

ASSOCIATE PUBLISHER
Jim Minatel

PROJECT COORDINATOR, COVER
Katie Crocker

COMPOSITOR
Chris Gillespie,
Happenstance Type-O-Rama

PROOFREADER
Jen Larsen, Word One

INDEXER
Robert Swanson

COVER IMAGE
Aaltazar / iStockPhoto

COVER DESIGNER
Ryan Sneed

Acknowledgments

We all have stories, and I would never in a million years have thought that my story would include the chapter "Published Author." The road to "this place" has never been dull. Through all the twists and turns in the path, I have been fortunate enough to have been surrounded by some truly fantastic people.

The staff of Wiley has been a great group of people with whom to collaborate. Mary James came to me with an idea for a book and supported me when I came back with a whole other approach; thus, this book was born. Ginny Munroe, my project manager, was responsible for guiding me through this new experience and has had to endure my journey as an aspiring writer. My technical editor, Barry Moltz, has passed on great wisdom that I have filed away. And, of course, Rosemarie Graham guided me back on track when I started to go off-road. Someone else I would like to give special thanks to is the busy Brian Solis of Altimeter Group, who carved out a chunk of time to write the Foreword for this book. I am very appreciative.

I have had the privilege to work with many fine people who have helped form my interest and drive in the social media field. Rick Calvert and Dave Cynkin of Blogworld Expo have been kind enough to have me speak at their west and east coast conferences several times over the last few years. I would not be where I am today without my time spent at Meshin (a Xerox innovation), LSF Interactive, Swivel Media, or my first real "gig" at this social media business with CC Chapman and Joseph Jaffe. I must also acknowledge Adam Curry for looking past the blond bombshell exterior of the avatar Britney Mason in *Second Life* and seeing more potential than others had.

My business partner, Kriselle Laran, at Bullfrog Media has been a great source of insight and feedback.

To all my clients, I say thank you for letting me be a part of what you are doing.

Those who follow me on either Facebook or Twitter and have mocked my bad spelling (I had an editor for this, ha!), answered the questions I put to you, directed me to great content, and continue to educate me daily.... I am grateful for your loyalty.

I am lucky to have a family that has allowed me to cultivate my new profession in social media. My father gave me space to continue work in the family business while pursuing this new line of work. My in-laws have been an excellent sounding board and a place I can turn to for solid advice.

My wife has encouraged me in my pursuits and been tolerant of my "moments of absence" from the family unit while attempting to write a book. I would like to thank my five children, who have always thought that what I am doing is "cool"—at least in the business world.

Because I seem to be moving in a backward timeline with my thanks, I would like to finally give a "shout out" to the youngest two children, for if they hadn't been so alert after their 4:30 a.m. feedings as newborns, I would never have started down this road.

Contents at a Glance

Contents

Foreword

The End of Business as Usual and the Beginning of a New Era of Connected Businesses

Twitter, Facebook, YouTube, Yelp, foursquare—it seems that every day, there's a new network capturing the attention of consumers everywhere. These social networks were once thought to be the playgrounds of the millennial. Now these networks dominate global headlines, changing the way that everyday people connect and communicate with one another. But that's just the beginning of where this story unfolds. Social networks are fundamentally transforming the way people find and share everything that's important to them.

Social media democratized information and empowered consumers to take control of not only their online experiences but also those in the real world. As a result, social media is changing how customers shop, refer products and services, and ultimately make decisions. The relationship between customers and business is changing and will continue to evolve as new media permeates our culture and society. What is important to understand is that this isn't a fad nor is any of this going to revert back to the way things used to be. Consumers are connected, entitled, and now expect recognition and value just to get their attention, let alone their business.

How We Got Here

A funny thing happened with social networks. People started sharing what they thought and did so vigorously. Although the extent of what people would say about brands, products, or services wasn't highly anticipated; it shouldn't have come as such a surprise. After all, businesses were subjected to customer opinions online going back to the early days of Web 1.0. With the likes of Amazon.com, epinions, and online peer-to-peer review systems, the voice of the consumer was given a stage and a magnificent theater to cast a spotlight on their experiences and expressions. Fanatical audiences could now come and go at will to hear what anyone and everyone said. More important, these audiences were captive—ready to take action based on what individuals had to say specifically related to brand and product decisions they were considering.

The difference between then and now is profound. Social media didn't invent the ability for customers to share their opinions, but it did amplify them. Consumer reviews are no longer stationary. With the rise of social networks, customer experiences are now portable and actionable. And as customers expanded their personal social networks, their experiences became exponentially influential. Now customers are empowered and connected, and their words affect the decisions of their peers in multiple networks. One experience can reside in Yelp, linger in foursquare, make the rounds in Facebook and Twitter, and come to life as a lasting record of events in blogs and YouTube. And because of the viral nature of social media, the ability to affect decisions is potentially infinite.

Social media is as intimidating as it is encouraging. Not only does it work for customers, but it also empowers businesses to learn from customer sentiment and adapt to their wants and needs. Social media is a window to relevance and the ability to compete for the future, today.

The Sky Is Not Falling; It Rains with Opportunity

I remember the early days of Yelp and the backlash that erupted among business owners outraged at the ability for customers to share negative experiences. The anger intensified as consumers flocked to the network en masse. "People will stop coming to our establishment," businesses would exclaim. "Customers are going to be swayed by the bad things some of our customers are saying," others feared.

To this day, I still have only one word to say in response, "Exactly."

Customers are now front and center of the business owner, forever changing how businesses think about the people they serve and why they deserve their support.

Social networks do not represent the end of your business. They do however symbolize the beginning of the end of business as usual. This is where your journey begins. It's not about fearing the ability for customers to share what's wrong; it's about building relationships and delivering meaningful experiences that inspire customers to share their take on why you are amazing.

Great experiences not only engender loyalty, they also serve as the catalysts for attracting new customers. The people who are connected to your customers will take action based on what they say. This is the promise and opportunity of social media.

Your customers now feel a sense of ownership in the businesses they support. As a result, you've now inherited a potent marketing force that pays for the privilege of doing business with you and, in turn, tells the world why.

I believe you are holding this book because you recognize that your customers are becoming more important to your business with every new connection they make. With this book, Dave Peck is handing you the keys to open the doors to social media and vibrant business opportunities. By engaging your connected customers, you by default become connected. Doing so shapes and reshapes online and offline experiences, bringing small businesses and local establishments to life in popular and incredibly active digital domains.

The reality of business is that customer experiences will either be positive or negative. The good news is that these experiences are yours to define. What they encounter and what they share within their networks is directly tied to your intentions, your investment in products and services, and the means used to deliver happiness and guarantee satisfaction.

Social media aside, the future of business is about improving relationships and customer experiences. To help, Dave has outlined how social media redefines the relationship between businesses and customers. And by the time you've finished this book, you will know everything necessary to build social campaigns and strategies that work. By asking the right questions, making informed decisions and using readily available tools, even the smallest business can be successful at engaging online.

This is your time to not just react to customer activity in social networks but create remarkable experiences that foster meaningful relationships. This is your time to lead, not follow.

Your customers are waiting.

—BRIAN SOLIS

Brian Solis is a business analyst and principal at Altimeter Group and the author of the award-wining *Engage!* and the *End of Business as Usual*.

Introduction

When a person or business wants to start an online marketing campaign, the most important part of this campaign is the use of social media sites. Services such as Facebook and Twitter are just what you need for virtually immediate dissemination of information at its widest and farthest coverage. Sites such as these enable people to speak in real time through chatting, commenting, and generally conversing, producing opportunities for instantaneous feedback and return on investment. Most of these sites don't charge premiums, helping businesses and individuals with limited budgets to do a lot with little financial investment.

Some businesses are so enthralled with the opportunity that they plunge into the experience without much planning. This is where many businesses and individuals make the biggest mistakes. Before diving in, it's necessary to take a step back to develop a strategy that can help drive the biggest return on investment. Even though the sites are typically free, the time invested in learning about these sites, developing a community, and nurturing relationships can add up to significant amounts. If you're spending time, you're spending money, whether you realize it. However, by taking the necessary steps and asking the right questions before starting the journey into social media marketing, the overall cost of being online can become little to none.

Look at Facebook. At the time of this writing, this social media site is closing in on 700 million users with accounts on its platform. When a business goes and creates a page for fans to visit, it's unlikely that advertising efforts on Facebook will go to waste with such a large audience to reach out to. However, because updates and posts are limited to those who are already within the administrator's friends list, a business or brand needs to strategize and develop more ways to reach other newsfeeds, such as through tagging, commenting on relevant topics, and engaging in useful conversations.

Blogs are also "in" nowadays. Although it does not require adding friends, the content is open to the public at large, and you can be followed by fellow bloggers. If content is always useful information that continues to engage readers, the blog has the potential to gain a good amount of online traffic in virtually no time.

Twitter has made a name for itself in terms of microblogging. Its 140-character limit on posts has infiltrated its way through the online subculture. It's changed the way people talk and write—in both positive and negative ways. Although it has certainly had a role in shortening attention spans and creating noise on the interwebs, it's also helped people to be more clear, concise, and efficient in communication. Twitter also opened up possibilities of new networking circles by making it easier to discover other people with similar interests. Information passes to people more quickly and over a wider geographical area. Relevant information that is also interesting will definitely be retweeted, and while millions of users do that, more attention is received by the source.

If you are asked again why you need *social media marketing* for your business, you will definitely know how to answer after reading this book. Currently, people are flocking to online communities, and if most of your target audience is participating, it's best to follow through and participate. Social media marketing is a type of marketing that involves the use of social networking and social mediums. It has become a daily part of both personal and professional lives, and has become a necessity for brands to thrive and grow. With compelling content coupled with a gripping title and a few facts, you can see that there are some substantial grounds why you should use social media marketing to grow your business.

Social Media Is Cost-Effective

Using social media and blogging are among the most cost-effective methods to reach your audience because these methods are, for the most part, free. The only thing it will cost you is your time; however, the quality of traffic that you can get in return compensates for it. If you are on a tight budget, social media marketing is definitely for you. Many self-described "experts" and "gurus" sell courses, and while some are actually valuable, you need to be aware that most are just not worth the money.

Social Media Saves Time

Contrary to popular belief, setting up a social media account is quick and self-explanatory. You can create a Facebook page today and set up a blog in a couple of hours. It will not take you all day on StumbleUpon to get good results.

With good planning and the right approach, you can get fantastic results with just a few hours per week on social media sites. I know of someone who spends a long time on a daily basis just to be a top Digg user; however you do not have to be a top Digg user to attract social media traffic. Avoid spending so much time on social networking sites just to drive traffic to your website when you can be tending to other aspects of your business.

Social Media Gets Quick Results and Instant Engagement

Building a website that is placed early in search results by search engines and with steady high traffic can take an extensive amount of time and effort, especially if it's a well-sought-after niche. However, with social media you can develop content and be seen by thousands of visitors giving you nearly instant market feedback— good and bad. Due to the potential for instant engagement, social media is an ideal option for getting a new website or blog noticed within hours.

Personal Branding and Website Traffic

Every business has a branding trading name; regardless of the size of the business, it is essential that business owners create distinctive and durable perceptions in the minds of their consumers to help position them as thought leaders.

As a result of exposure available through social media, it is easy for business owners to create their branding online. Social media marketing is a free option for persistently creating a unique business identity. As you network with individuals on social networking sites, you create some kind of impression (hopefully good).

Social media sites are excellent ways to get visitors to come to your website. Links to your website from social networking websites can improve your search engine ranking positions that can consequently generate click-through targeted visitors to your website.

Reading this book can help individuals and businesses building personal and corporate brands to ask the right questions and get the right tools, tips, and tricks to create a strong and engaging online presence.

Planning a Brand

In this chapter:

- 1. Why do I need to establish a brand?
- 2. Brand, online presence—what's the difference?
- 3. What are some successful brands?
- 4. How do I develop my brand strategy?
- 5. What is my brand's objective?
- 6. Who is my target audience?
- 7. Am I reflecting my brand?

Importance

1. Why Do I Need to Establish a Brand?

In this day of everyone wanting to be the next expert, thought leader, and YouTube star, creating a personal brand is more important than ever. Now, before you take a deep-breath sigh thinking, "Where do I begin with this?" or "It sounds like too much work," you need to realize that you probably already have one!

Put this book down and go to your computer. Go to Google and type in your name and city. If you have a website or a LinkedIn, Facebook, YouTube, or Twitter account, it will come up in the search. Amazing, right? All this information about you or your brand is already out there on the Internet. It is nearly impossible to get it taken off, deleted, or removed. What you can do is take control and manage your personal brand, making it so people can find and learn the things about you that you want them to know.

Establishing your brand online is a necessary step in your overall marketing plan. More than ever, people find themselves online looking for information or entertainment. Whether the brand represents large corporations, startups, or individuals, it acts as a voice or personification of that business.

In social media, a brand is more important than ever. Without a developed brand, companies and individuals would have no focus in their marketing outreach. People wouldn't connect with companies because they wouldn't find a common ground, and return on investment in social media would be minimal. Social media services and sites are readily available for brands to have online support for many different functions, including video, networking, accounting, and more.

A brand is more than a name. A name may identify a company or individual, but it doesn't actually hold any meaning for the consumer. The brand (or personality) is what helps people to understand what the company is all about. Some of the many social networking sites available for brands include Facebook, LinkedIn, StumbleUpon It!, Yahoo!, Twitter, YouTube, and so on.

> When first starting to develop your brand, start with your logo tagline and mission statement to generate ideas for your strategy.

Related Questions

➜ 12. What social networks best fit my goals? **Page 40**

➜ 75. How can social media websites make this easier? **Page 212**

➜ 77. Why does what I do in the real world matter? **Page 216**

Rule of Thumb In social media, personality is the key to success. If you have to use your business name as your brand name online, be sure to add a human touch by letting people know who it is that is speaking on behalf of the company.

Action Item

➜ If you do show up on a Google search, write down what page your information is listed on in the search results, and note the order in which your information is listed. Knowing your Google search ranking is useful when you work on improving your website presence so that you have a baseline to start.

Importance

2. Brand or Online Presence—What's the Difference?

Determining the answer to "What is a brand?" can be a tough question to ask. Many companies cannot seem to answer the question in a straightforward manner.

Walter Landor, well known in the advertising industry, said, "Simply put, a brand is a promise. By identifying and authenticating a product or service, it delivers a pledge of satisfaction and quality."

Walter summed it up nicely, but today it can mean so much more. Today, it can be also seen as "A collection of perceptions in the mind of the consumer." This is exactly what you want to create online.

In March 2010, I spoke at the South by Southwest (SXSW) Interactive Conference in Austin, Texas. The topic was "How to Score a Job" using social networking. The room was full of job recruiters. They shared that they put a heavy emphasis on applicants' online presence. By online presence, I am essentially referring to how active one is on the Web with personal websites, blogs, published articles, activities on programming forums, and so on. One recruiter went as far as to say that, when hiring for technical positions, he would ignore applicants who although fully qualified, lacked the online presence that someone with their skills should have. If you're a Ruby on Rails programmer, there's no better way to show your passion for the framework than by blogging about it, publishing tips and guides, or simply helping others work with it. Companies can easily see that, which definitely helps during the interviewing and selection process.

Alternatively, having an online presence can pose a negative. People often find false comfort in privacy and security settings for the various networks, and post content that can reflect negatively on a brand. Putting up pictures of the night's drunken escapades or venting about a coworker may not bode well for business the next day. Online presence is simply the act of being online. By having ways for people to search and find you online, you establish a presence.

> SXSW is a series of films, interactive festivals, music festivals, and conferences that take place every spring in Austin, Texas.

Related Questions

Action Items

➜ Visit every site on which your brand has a presence and clean up any content that may be deemed negative or controversial by others (unless you want the controversial image).

➜ Immediately after setting up your profile on a social network, visit the privacy settings and customize them to what works best for your needs.

Importance

3. What Are Some Successful Brands?

Regardless of whether you are a person, a small business, or a big business, you have one thing in common: you're a brand. You want your brand to be successful and well known. This section looks at what some big brands have done to expand their online presence using social media.

Starbucks

Starbucks coffee chain (see Figure 1-1) likes to post what it calls "freshly brewed tweets" to its Twitter following of more than 1.3 million. If you look at the number of tweets that this brand does, you might notice a certain trend. What you see is a large number of engaging replies and mentions to its community almost every day. Starbucks has a strong reputation for being engaging and talking to people on Twitter. It doesn't just sell coffee.

Starbucks understands what it means for a brand to engage with its customers. All too often brands use Twitter to "shout" or spam their followers with relentless sales talk and ads—all the while without caring to respond to mentions or direct messages by their followers. Sure, Starbucks does post the occasional promo or new offer, but the brand's use of Twitter is mainly to connect intimately with fans and customers.

The online presence that Starbucks has developed reflects its offline brand. It listens and has caused people to start conversations about the brand, and that results in brand loyalty and revenue.

Ford

Scott Monty is the head of the social media movement at Ford Motor Company. He is what some consider the main "driving force" responsible for adding an entirely new dimension of social media savvy to this historic and world-recognized brand.

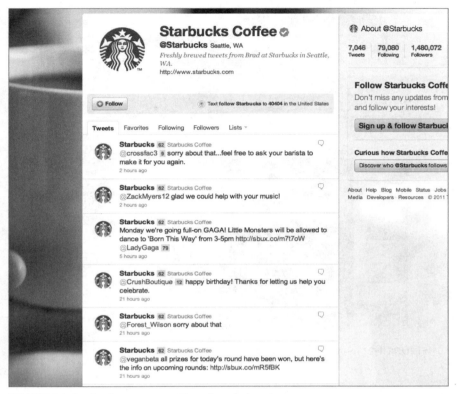

FIGURE 1-1: Starbucks connects with its fans and customers.

Not only does Ford engage on Twitter, Facebook, and YouTube, it has taken social media into the real world. The Ford Fiesta Movement (see Figure 1-2) is a campaign aimed directly at "Millennials," the driving youth born between 1979 and 1995. This campaign consists of 100 "trendsetters" who basically kept a Ford Fiesta for six months and blogged or talked on social networks about their experiences with the vehicle. YouTube video applications to take part in this campaign were accepted and generated so much positive buzz that Ford initiated the Ford Focus Movement only one year later. With campaigns such as the Ford Fiesta Movement and Ford Focus Movement, Scott has changed the social media game.

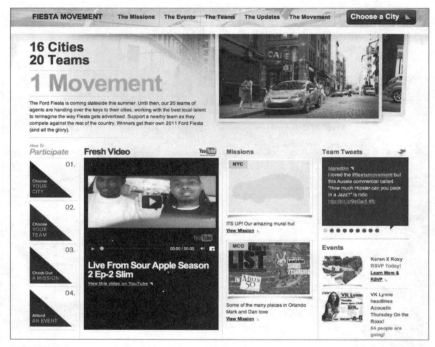

FIGURE 1-2: The Ford Fiesta Movement campaign

By doing these online/real-world campaigns, Ford enables its brand to become, well, more human, in a way. The brand engages with customers, evokes people's emotions, and takes part in conversations.

Dell

Dell has a lot of Twitter accounts (see Figure 1-3) —I do mean a lot. Something like more than 90. You might think that with that many Twitter accounts, its social media movement would be a mess. That just is not the case. Many key people at the company are tweeting about the day-to-day activities and what their division is doing, from Chairman and CEO Michael Dell to support staff like @richardatdell. Dell continues to gain advocates through Twitter because it's not just coupons and exclusive promos it tweets about. At the heart of the company's huge network on Twitter is a focus to keep the conversations about its brand going. The key to its success is engagement with its customers on a personal and human level.

FIGURE 1-3: Dell segments its social media efforts to help ensure that they reach every possible consumer need, from customer service to technical support to general outreach.

> ? Dell earned more than $3 million in revenue thanks to its strong Twitter presence in 2009.

Comcast

Bill Gerth is the man running Comcast's Twitter account at @Comcast Cares. I know this because, well, it is listed right there. Oh—and in February 2011, I had a personal experience where I turned to Twitter for help...or, rather, to vent.

Unable to communicate my need and issue to the customer service representative, I tweeted to express my unhappiness. Within a minute, @ComcastCares saw my Tweet. He quickly found the service ticket and reviewed the case and the breakdown in communication I had with the CSR. He contacted me, fixed the problem, and most important, he saved my account. See Figure 1-4.

Even though Comcast is a huge cable operator and broadband Internet service provider, it "gets" social media. Why? Because, as you can see with my own personal case, it isn't too big to pay attention to customers and their issues.

FIGURE 1-4: Comcast's social media support team has worked hard to transform a negative brand sentiment into something seen as very positive in the social space.

Frank Eliason was the original man behind @ComcastCares, and it is largely due to him that Comcast has developed such a positive brand sentiment within social media. He worked with his team to take a company known largely for having a negatively perceived brand, and created such a customer service presence online that Comcast is now viewed as one of the most socially respected.

Southwest Airlines

In 2009, on my way back home to California from Austin, Texas, I had a delayed JetBlue flight. Wanting to know how long the delay would be, I approached the counter. Getting no straight answer for whether it was

10 minutes or 10 hours, I went to Twitter for a little customer support. Having a Twitter conversation with @jetblue (see Figure 1-5) went well at first. That was until it did not get back to me on Twitter for an hour. Within that time frame, it seems Southwest Airlines was watching the conversation I was having with JetBlue and decided to join in.

FIGURE 1-5: JetBlue Twitter Conversation

Southwest quickly offered me a quick-and-direct flight home from Austin. Not only did it attempt to steal business from JetBlue using Twitter, it also created a huge buzz by doing it—with more than 200 retweets about it, numerous blog posts, and case studies.

Rule of Thumb Always be careful about what you say and do online. Even if you think you are deleting, it is always out there.

Many of the examples listed here show how customer service can succeed in social media. Other ways to use social media are marketing, PR, and general outreach.

Related Questions

➤ 42. What should I tweet about? **Page 120**

➤ 48. What should my fan page be about? **Page 141**

➤ 52. How do Facebook "likes" help me? **Page 150**

➤ 77. Why does what I do in the real world matter? **Page 216**

Action Items

➤ Study other successful brands online and listen to what they have to say online. They can act as guides in your mission to develop your brand's online presence.

➤ Check out your competitors and see what they are doing online. Note what works for you and what doesn't.

4. How Do I Develop My Brand Strategy?

Importance

Defining your brand is the first step to develop your branding strategy. Your brand definition can serve as your measuring stick in evaluating any and all marketing materials and strategies. You need to ask the following key questions to help define your brand:

- ➦ What products and services do you offer? Define the qualities of these services and products.

- ➦ What are the core values of your products and services? What are the core values of your company?

- ➦ What is your mission?

- ➦ What is your specialty?

- ➦ Who is your target market?

- ➦ Who do your products and services attract?

- ➦ What is the tagline of your company?

- ➦ What message does your tagline send to your prospects?

Rule of Thumb   Consider your target audience when answering each question.

By answering these questions, you can begin to create a personality or character for your brand that represents your products or services. What is the character like? What qualities stand out? Is the personality of your brand innovative, creative, energetic, or sophisticated?

Using this personality, you can then begin to build a relationship with your target market. How does that personality react to a target audience? What characteristics stand out? Which characteristics and qualities get the attention of your prospects?

The Four Cs: Clarity, Consistency, Continuity, and Creativity

Successful brands of all types have the following four characteristics: clarity, consistency, continuity, and creativity.

CLARITY

Your audience is bombarded with thousands of messages every day, and for yours to break through the clutter and have the desired impact, you need to be clear about what you want to say. You need to answer the question, "What single idea should someone remember from engaging with you?" Are you an expert in accounting? Travel? Discounts? Being a mom? Assuming that you can only tell someone one thing about yourself, product, or service, exactly what would it be? Now, focus on that; highlight that single thing, and you have clarity. Avoid the temptation to try to tell everyone everything.

What action do you want the reader, viewer, or listener to take? Should they visit your website, call you, or stop by the office? Never assume that they will know what to do or what you want them to do.

When you combine a clear message with a clear call to action, you dramatically increase the odds of success. And clarity is simple—give your audience a reason to take action and give them an action to take. Clarity leads to success.

CONSISTENCY

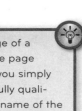

A home page of a website is the page displayed if you simply type in the fully qualified domain name of the site in the address bar of your browser and press Enter. For instance, when you type in www.cnn.com and press Enter in the address bar, you go to CNN's home page.

Brand consistency is important in marketing and social media. You need to communicate messages in a way that doesn't detract or wander away from your core brand proposition. For example, a single logo is always used in a similar way on all social networking sites and with similar typeface, color, and design styles so that everything visual is interlinked and has a link back to your home page. A network is like a member of the same family, supporting and even looking similar to all the other members in the family. Your brand needs to have its own unique "look and feel," which enables a person to recognize it as belonging to your brand, making it unique.

It is about ensuring that all the messaging of all networks have the same look and feel—that it all "looks" consistent.

Brand consistency has one massive advantage, which is recognition. With recognition comes familiarity. With familiarity comes trust and confidence. Also, if done correctly, consistency brings clarity and purpose that consumers buy into. They can become loyal. Often people don't like "new"—and it has been widely reported that before consumers purchase a product, on average, they need to be exposed to a brand 17 times. Seventeen times is a tremendous amount, so it's essential that when potential customers come across a "brand message," they know straight away which brand is communicating to them. This can be done only with consistency. If consistency is not applied, and the message and design are not defined, consumers might mistake one brand with a competing brand, which could then mean they associate the impression with another company. This means a business potentially loses customers and may even help its competitors if a consistent "look" and tone are not achieved.

The unique "look" of your brand might evolve slowly over time, but your core message should never actually change. Take, for example, Apple computers. Since its brand's conception, its brand proposition was to supply advanced, quality, great looking, and high-performing computers. This message has never changed; however, the way it has communicated this over the years has changed because the way people consume and interact with brands has changed. This has led to consumer recognition and then trust and loyalty from its customers.

The issue is that brand consistency often takes many years to master before it can start to work for you. This means you need to think long term. Leading brands are normally leading because they have had many years of consistency behind them and they have had a long-term goal for their branding, which has been consistent. The trick is to have in place a clear idea of your brand.

Those who manage marketing and communication efforts as a series of individual projects rather than a campaign often overlook consistency in brand strategy. Consistency means that you deliver the same message across all channels: your website, Facebook, Twitter, and all others.

If the message you want to deliver is that you are the best and most-unique used car dealership in the industry, you need to sell it! Use every opportunity to remind your audience that you are the best in that industry. Quickly your clients and future clients will start to believe that message.

CONTINUITY

Like consistency, continuity helps to ensure that the brand message is properly portrayed throughout all the different ways consumers can come into contact with the brand. Marketing efforts are more than just online efforts; they also deal with everything offline such as the name, logo, business materials (letterhead, business cards, and so on), email signatures, website, calls to action, and sales materials.

Continuity in messaging helps bring consumers from point to point without losing understanding of what your brand is trying to say. Every piece of your brand should strive to communicate a continuous message.

CREATIVITY

This type of creative branding addresses all four Cs: clarity, consistency, continuity, and creativity.

Although last, creativity is by no means the least important. A brand message should capture the attention of its potential consumers. Following the lead of other brands can be useful in terms of generating ideas, but the most successful social media campaigns often come from the brands that step out of the box. Being creative in marketing and messaging can help to reach consumers previously marked as unreachable.

Related Questions

➤ 16. What should I use as a website address? **Page 62**

➤ 18. Is a logo important? **Page 66**

➤ 88. What does a social media strategy look like? **Page 244**

➤ 97. How can I build influence? **Page 258**

Action Item

→ Document your strategy and include it in your general marketing or business plan. Every person on the team should know what the strategy of social media is so that there is no possibility of conflict or issue.

Importance

5. What Is My Brand's Objective?

Critical to effective brand management is the clear definition of the brand's audience and the objectives that the brand needs to achieve. What are the objectives that you hope to achieve with your brand? Is it to offer customer service? Is it to retain customers? Is it to get customers? Maybe it is to drive brand awareness?

Your brand should be composed of the brand's personality, image, core competencies, and characteristics. The impressions that you make and the words people use to describe your brand to others are the basic framework of your brand.

With a strong brand, you build credibility and more influence on your market, and you can motivate customers and clients to purchase from you. If done correctly, you will be looked at as a thought leader, not a follower.

By defining your objectives with specific timelines, it is easier to develop a plan of action to achieve those objectives. By defining your objectives, you can map out a plan for how to achieve these objectives. For example, your objective is to position yourself as a thought leader in insurance. How can you go about doing this? You can:

- → Have members of your team speak at trade shows.
- → Schedule lectures at professional group gatherings within your industry.
- → Write and publish regular blog posts.
- → Create a website to host and share knowledge.
- → Incite discussions via social media such as on Twitter, Facebook, or LinkedIn.
- → Answer questions on Quora to show your expertise.

After you determine your objectives, the next step is to build and develop your brand strategy by listing how, when, and what you are going to do to accomplish and meet your brand's objectives.

Rule of Thumb   Your actions online should all be made with brand objectives in mind.

Related Questions

➤ 1. Why do I need a personal brand? **Page 2**

➤ 4. How do I develop my brand strategy? **Page 13**

➤ 10. How do I brand my online identity? **Page 34**

➤ 97. How can I build influence? **Page 258**

Action Items

To determine your brand's objectives, document the answers to the following questions:

➤ What is it that you want your brand to offer people?

➤ What do you want others to know and say about your products or services?

Importance

6. Who Is My Target Audience?

Your value proposition must be relevant to your target market. This means your target market must be clearly defined. It's not uncommon for a business to need to refocus and revisit what it's targeting, especially if it is not clearly identified in the beginning stages of business.

You need to find the right balance when defining your target market so that your audience can recognize that you are talking specifically to them. This often requires companies to narrow their target market.

Why Is Your Target Market Important in Branding?

Regardless of what your brand is missing, gaining the devotion of your target audience is necessary to reach those objectives.

To achieve your brand marketing goals, you need to know your target market inside and out. This requires conducting a market analysis. This market analysis must be as in depth as possible, providing you with all the data you need to effectively reach your target. By knowing your target audience, you can be confident in the steps to take to connect with that audience.

The power of your brand relies on your ability to focus. That is why defining your target market can help to strengthen your brand's effectiveness. The best way to do this is to conduct an informal market analysis of your target market and write a target audience summary for your brand.

Conduct Your Informal Market Analysis

Make your study as complete as possible. Use the Internet to conduct research. You can also read news stories related to your target market. This can help you to narrow down your target by interest, demographic, and common trends.

Following are some important questions to ask that will help you through the process of completing this analysis.

➔ Who is your target audience?

➔ Where is your target audience located?

➔ What do audience members think about your current brand?

➔ What would you like your audience to think about your brand?

➔ How will you attract them to your products or services?

➔ Who else is competing for their loyalty and devotion?

➔ Are you targeting business or consumer sectors?

Interacting with your target market doesn't stop at asking questions. Engage with your prospects in other ways, too. Read their blogs and comment on them. Give them a call. Set up an appointment to go talk to them. Interact with them via other social media tools. Listen to what they're saying. Make yourself known to them. You never know when a simple conversation will lead to a long-lasting, mutually beneficial working relationship.

 Rule of Thumb   Your target market should be on the social networks on which you want to have a presence.

Related Questions

➔ 41. How do I increase my Twitter following? **Page 117**

➔ 49. How do I get people to like my fan page? **Page 143**

➔ 62. What are contacts and can I have too many? **Page 172**

➔ 91. How do I figure out who my key influences are? **Page 248**

Action Item

➔ Using a spreadsheet application, list the different demographics that comprise your target market and the ways you are planning to reach out to them. You can use this spreadsheet as a foundation for a statistical dashboard to track your ROI later.

Importance

7. Am I Reflecting My Brand?

Branding is your identity in the marketplace. Is yours saying what it should? Your company image is about the appearance of your packaging. What is your company image saying to the marketplace?

Packaging always either has a negative or positive influence on the purchaser. A negative impression can detour a potential customer, just as a positive reaction can influence a customer to buy. A time to pay special attention to your packaging is when you are in the launch of a "new" brand. If you've already built a strong brand that others recognize, often people may not pay as close attention to the packaging.

How can you package your brand so that it is an integral part of your business and represents a strong identity? Keep in mind that I am not speaking of packaging as a traditional box that contains a product, but as a vehicle that reflects your company's brand and image. Packaging can be judged and represented by the following common business tools:

➧ Business cards and stationery

➧ Website

➧ Email address

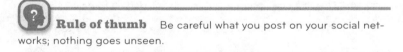

Rule of thumb   Be careful what you post on your social networks; nothing goes unseen.

What image are you putting across social networking sites that you use every day? What do people say about your company? Take the time to look at how your brand is perceived.

What are your business cards and stationery saying? Are they saying you are strong, you are confident, you are a thought leader, and you offer unique services? Or do they reflect an image that says you are flimsy and not dynamic and you will try but cannot guarantee continuity?

What does your website say about your company? Does it reflect professionalism and clarity? Does it show viewers that you respect and care about them? Or does your website confuse viewers, project an untrustworthy image of your company, and ultimately drive potential customers away?

What does your email address say about your company? Does it suggest your role in the company, is it easy to remember, and does it say something about you and your business? Or does it project a meaningless or generic emptiness? If you use the email address funandsexy@aol.com to email people from your accounting business, it is time to get a new one.

Lastly, are you (or your team) reflecting your brand properly? Every word and action made by someone on your team can affect how the public views your brand. If you have people from your team on Twitter that make it known they are a part of your brand, you really want to make sure that expectations are properly set, in writing, so that there aren't issues later on. This is all a part of your social media strategy. The strategy should include your brand's "do's and don'ts" so that everyone involved understand what is okay and what is not okay to post online.

This doesn't just apply to Twitter. LinkedIn, Facebook, any social outlet that a team member can be on is subject to public scrutiny. If Jane from Accounting goes out with her friends on Saturday night, you may want to be sure she understands that posting drunken pictures on her Facebook page, which by the way happens to indicate that she's a part of the ABC Brand network, is not going to be okay on Monday morning when she gets to the office...unless, of course, your brand specializes in bachelor/bachelorette parties in Vegas.

> If you or a member of your team has a personal account on Twitter, you might want to include a disclaimer on your background or bio that indicates your thoughts and postings don't reflect those of your employer or company.

As you can see, all these things speak volumes about your image and either strengthen or weaken your brand. Your image is all in the packaging. Would potential clients take a second look, or is your message getting lost? If you thought these things were not worth the investment or didn't matter, you were wrong. Clients and customers make both subconscious and public assessments of your company based on these things and that customer appraisal says much about your business, your attitude, and your priorities.

Related Questions

→ 5. Why is my brand's objective? **Page 18**

→ 77. Why does what I do in the real world matter? **Page 216**

→ 95. How often should I update my strategy? **Page 254**

→ 98. How can I keep my social media efforts interesting? **Page 261**

Action Item

→ In the social networking world, you need to build a solid reputation. As an example, JetBlue does a lot of its customer support through its Twitter account. After helping someone, it always makes sure it thanks people for following its account on Twitter and flying. Doing something like this is a great way to build your reputation.

Building an Online Identity

In this chapter:

?

Importance

8. What Is a Username?

A username is the name that represents your online profile on a social networking site. It is usually the first thing that people notice about you, and it is a good idea to choose a unique and identifiable username to make yourself stand out from the crowd and draw attention. As a result, your username should be creative and should be something that represents you and your personality and interests in some way.

It is important to remember the importance of a username, especially with a platform such as Twitter where most people check a username before even looking at your profile. Therefore, you should choose a username to attract users to your profile. So, it pays to be as creative as possible when choosing a username. With this is mind, just how can you be creative and choose a username that hasn't already been taken?

The first thing to think about is that it should be memorable, so keep it short and catchy. If you need to be easily found on a platform, you might consider using your first name as part of your username to make it easy for friends, family, or peers to find you. If the platform you use is character-limited, keep your username short, so as not to take up too much space away from other content.

If you are using your business name to develop your brand, it should be easier to establish your username on a site. If you find that someone else is already using it or your full business name is too long, see what else you can use that still represents your company. For example, Southwest Airlines uses @southwestair, which both represents their company and abbreviates a word to save character space.

> **Rule of Thumb**   A site such as Twitter limits the number of characters (letters, numbers, and symbols) you can put into a reply. It is a good thing to have a short username; it allows for more space for the response.

Don't try to be too clever or go for difficult-to-pronounce tongue twisters because this can make it difficult for you to tell other people what your username is, or for them to remember or understand it.

> If your real name is taken, use a picture of yourself for your avatar. That way your friends or peers will know it's you even if they don't recognize your username.

Following are key to choosing a username:

- **Don't be afraid to use your real name**—There's nothing wrong with using your name on Twitter. If you use Twitter as a networking tool or an opportunity to connect with others for personal or professional enrichment, calling yourself DarthVader918345 isn't the smartest decision. Use your real name and maintain your branding. Those you communicate with will appreciate it.

- **Don't use curse words or obscenity in your username**—It's not common, but I've come across people who decide to add curse words or suggestive concepts into their username. I don't get it. People who actually want to contribute something to the community shouldn't use their username as a vehicle to shock others.

- **Do tell us about your profession or your interests**—If you're using Twitter to expand your professional network, you can use your username to tell us what you do. If you're a plumber, say so. If you're an attorney, tell us. There's no better way to attract followers than to give them a hint about who you are. If your followers know you're a plumber, maybe they'll ask you how to unclog a drain. Even better, maybe they'll ask if they can hire you to fix their plumbing problem. For personal users, if you're a gamer, say so in your username. If you love PCs, we want to know it. Every time I see someone who puts SFGiantsfan or something like it in their username, I follow them because I know that we have something in common. There's nothing better than to have a Twitter dialogue with someone who shares your interests.

- **Do be creative**—If your preferred username is taken and you don't want to use your name, be creative. Make it meaningful. Make it funny. Do something that interests people. It'll pay off. Some great examples: Adventuregirl and MissDestructo.

- **Do distinguish yourself**—Clyde29 and Clyde85 might as well be the same person to me. If your username is similar to another person's username, your audience will probably have trouble distinguishing between the two of you. You don't know the taken usernames before you sign up, but don't just add a bunch of numbers after your name. That's so "2005."

➤ **Don't look like a automated computer robot**—The seasoned Twitter user can spot a "bot" in seconds. Usually these usernames are generic business names or an obvious scam, such as "MakeMoneyNow." Even if you're legitimately offering services or information, don't use a name like that; it doesn't tell us about you, and it makes us wonder whether or not you have purely commercial motives.

➤ **Don't use a celebrity's name unless it's your name, too**— Impersonating a celebrity is building yourself using another person's brand. Don't do it. Nobody likes it and nobody is going to fall for it.

➤ **Do consider impact**—How will your chosen username affect the way other users view you? Will they want to talk to you after they see your username? Will they immediately block you? Picking a username isn't as simple as choosing the first word that comes to mind. You need to decide what kind of impact you want it to have and go from there. If you want to insult, you'll have no trouble. If you want to show your loyalty to someone or something, go for it. Either way, the username you choose will affect the community in some way. Make it positive.

Examples of good usernames are

➤ iJustine

➤ lulugrimm

➤ adventuregirl

➤ barrymoltz

Examples of not-so-good usernames include

➤ Hoeser291242

➤ lovemachine

➤ bigmoneyperkins

➤ Barry_Moltz

If you absolutely have to use a spacer, such as a hyphen or underscore, use the hyphen. Search engines read hyphens like spaces and will read the full term as separate words. Underscores connect words together, and search engines cannot read the separate words.

Rule of Thumb   Twitter allows underscores in your user-name, but not hyphens. Facebook allows hyphens. Refrain from using either. It's easy for other people to forget these special characters when typing or recommending your profile to others.

Related Questions

➤ 7. Am I reflecting my brand? **Page 22**

➤ 10. How do I brand my online identity? **Page 34**

➤ 16. What should I use as a website address? **Page 62**

➤ 69. What keywords do I use? **Page 193**

Action Items

➤ Make a list of your top five preferred usernames.

➤ Go to each social site in which you plan to take part and check each to see if any of these usernames are available.

➤ Use the username that is available across all of the sites.

Importance

9. What Is an Avatar?

An avatar is a personalized graphic file or rendering that represents a computer user. There are basically two types of avatars: those used at websites, such as on Web exchange boards, and those used in gaming and virtual worlds.

The simplest type of avatar is a small graphics file used on websites. Websites that offer chat boards often enable members to upload an avatar to represent them. The avatar can be a real-life digital photo of the person using it, but is more often an image intended to be a creative alter ego. This might be a game-rendered snapshot of a beast, hero, or heroine; a humorous picture of a pet or cartoonish character; or a design that makes a statement. The avatar appears alongside the user's posts, easily identifying the author for others at a glance.

Your Twitter avatar will be square. You can use your business logo or your picture, but make sure everything fits well inside a square (see Figure 2-1).

> **?** A personal LinkedIn profile should be a headshot. A business page on LinkedIn can contain the business logo as the avatar.

FIGURE 2-1: Twitter can have customized background images that will help for adding information that you can't place on an avatar.

A Facebook avatar should be prepared while keeping in mind that a square image of the avatar will be used throughout the network, but a larger version can be used on the actual Facebook page (see Figure 2-2).

FIGURE 2-2: On Facebook, you can take advantage of a rectangular profile picture area to place added information that you want people to see.

Sometimes, a website offers a generic pool of avatars for those who have not yet created one. Commonly, the users replace the generic avatar as soon as they learn how to create a personal one. Many websites offer services that provide instructions for how to create and upload them.

Be sure to follow these guidelines:

➔ Have a professional or a dedicated amateur take your picture.

➔ Use a white background, or at least a solid-colored one. No trees! No snowstorms! This helps you stand out against the backdrop.

➔ The idea of having your significant other in the picture is a good one, at least in terms of maintaining peace in the presence of a jealous or nervous spouse. But people aren't friending your girl-friend; they are friending you. Make the picture a solo.

➔ If you wear a hat, you better have both a good reason and a good hat.

✦ Conceptual photos (such as your foot or a monkey wearing glasses) might give us insight into the real you, but perhaps you should save that insight for the second impression.

✦ How beautiful you are is a distant second to how happy you are. Photos that communicate openness and enthusiasm are far more appealing than photos that make you look like a supermodel.

✦ Cropping is important. A well-cropped photo sends an important subliminal message to other people. Cropping is the positioning of the image within its size boundaries. Most photographers and artists work off what is called the "rule of thirds" where the subject matter within a photo is either one-third or two-thirds of the full photograph. Proper cropping and position of the photo gives it so much more visual interest and will capture more attention than a poorly cropped image. If you don't know how to do this, browse through the work of professionals to see how they do it. It matters.

✦ Some people have started adding words or signs to their images. If your goal is to communicate that you are the website or you are the company, this is smart. If not, remember the cocktail party rule: If you wouldn't wear it there, don't wear it here.

Rule of Thumb   Be consistent. Because followers and friends look for your face first, it's important that once you find a photo that works, stick with it throughout all the networks on which you develop a presence.

Don't change it every few days. Don't even change it every month; just find one and go with it. People's attention is split a million different ways these days, and you get only a split second to try to make an impression and forge a connection. Consistency makes that easier.

This may be especially true for Twitter, where networks tend to go beyond personal friends and family.

Your profile is your personal brand and with any brand, consistency is key. When you market yourself, your avatar becomes your logo. It will be seen on everything.

Related Questions

➧ 7. Am I reflecting my brand? **Page 22**

➧ 10. How do I brand my online identity? **Page 34**

➧ 18. Is a logo important? **Page 66**

➧ 76. Do I still need a business card? **Page 214**

Action Items

➧ Pull together the images you intend to use for your avatar. Ensure proper branding by utilizing the same pieces on each site, with slight variations depending on the network size requirements. Look at the various avatars side by side before placing them online, for quality assurance.

➧ Save all of the avatars at 72 DPI to ensure proper web resolution. Ask your web designer or developer for help with this if you need it.

Importance

10. How Do I Brand My Online Identity?

The easiest ways to maintain branding efforts for online identities is to focus first on the name. Consistent usernames throughout the various social sites can help to curb confusion among followers and create efficiencies in messaging.

When you establish the same username on all of your sites, people will remember you more easily. If someone is following you on Twitter, he'll know that he can likely find you by searching for the same username on Facebook or LinkedIn. The easier you make it for people to find you, the more successful your social media campaign will be because you will simply have more people aware of and following your brand.

The avatar, your marketing message, and your general content are also a big part of how you brand yourself online. By establishing a solid and cohesive online strategy that aligns with your general marketing plan, you'll ensure that what you do online to establish your brand matches what you're doing offline.

In general, branding is what you do to your individual or business to increase public recognition and make sure that people know who you are and what you are about. Because the act of branding is supposed to make you recognizable, you want to be sure that everything you do with your online presence is an effort toward that goal. If you miss a step in the branding process or don't follow the stated path to your goals, you run the risk of damaging your brand by making it more difficult for people to remember it or making people question its authority or expertise. Either way can result in a negative return on your investment, and will make the efforts you place on your online presence damaging to your overall brand.

Rule of Thumb   Keeping usernames and avatars the same across all the network sites is the easiest way to support your branding efforts online.

Related Questions

➜ 8. What is a username? **Page 26**

➜ 11. Why does an email address matter? **Page 11**

➜ 76. Do I still need a business card? **Page 214**

➜ 77. Why does what I do in the real world matter? **Page 216**

Action Item

➜ If you are already on networks that don't have the same usernames, try to change them now. Twitter allows you to change your username as frequently as desired. Facebook allows you to change your username as long as you have less than 100 "fans" or "likes."

Importance

11. Why Does An Email Address Matter?

An email address is one of the most important tools a brand can have. It's a widely accepted form of communication that consumers can use at any given day or time. Less expensive than phones and more efficient than regular mail, email can be used to hold and develop long conversations.

Email addresses are also commonly used for access into protected or membership-only website features. Using an email address for sign-in purposes helps websites to vet users and make sure that they don't have duplicate content.

Using free services can lessen credibility for a brand. The continuity of a brand breaks and may cause confusion for consumers. Also, some free email services are known for spam accounts, which can cause your emails to fail spam filters when sending to people with strict email security settings.

Another benefit to using your own domain for email is that you can better guarantee availability of a desired username. In a small company, a first name for an email address will be easy to obtain and easy to communicate to customers. My email address is dave@bullfrog-media.com, which lets me maximize the use of my personal brand while promoting my business brand. Plus, saying "dave at bullfrog" is a lot easier than saying "david underscore peck 2345 exclamation mark at Yahoo."

By using an email address with your branded website address, you help to create a sense of openness as you allow consumers to have another avenue of communication with your brand.

> Many website hosting providers include email as a bonus for no additional cost.

Rule of Thumb   In general, the rule of thumb is to avoid putting your email address on your website. If you absolutely must put an email address on your website, use a generic email address such as info@, or, spell out the @ symbol by typing [at]. Spam bots often screen websites for the email addresses to collect for various purposes, so making use of alternate ways of contact on your website will help prevent spam emails. Whenever possible, use a contact form instead of an email address to prevent this issue.

Related Questions

➤ 8. What is a username? **Page 26**

➤ 10. How do I brand my online identity? **Page 34**

➤ 16. What should I use as a website address? **Page 62**

➤ 84. How do I prevent spam? **Page 234**

Action Items

➤ Check with your website hosting provider for email hosting plans. If you don't already have a free plan included with your account, get one.

➤ Activate your email account and then forward emails from your existing email address to this new address.

➤ Send notification to your business associates or clients to let them know of the change.

Choosing the Right Social Networks

Importance

12. What Social Networks Best Fit My Goals?

A social network is a website or network of websites specifically established to enable end users to communicate or connect on topics of mutual interest. These networks can address many different needs, and use of them varies depending on what you want to accomplish.

Before deciding what network works best for your goals, you have to take a look at the different existing services and see what they can offer. Social networks, or a form of them, have been around a lot longer than people realize, dating back to the late 1970s. The following sections discuss some of the milestones of the social networking timeline.

Usenet

Usenet systems (see Figure 3-1) were first conceived in 1979 by Tom Truscott and Jim Ellis. Usenet enables users to post articles or posts (referred to as *news*) to newsgroups. Usenet systems had no centralized server or dedicated administrator to set them apart from most Bulletin Board Systems (BBSes) and forums. Usenets are mostly responsible for the development of newsreader clients, which are the precursor to RSS feed readers so commonly used to follow blogs and news sites today. Group sites such as Google Groups and Yahoo! groups are our modern-day Usenet systems.

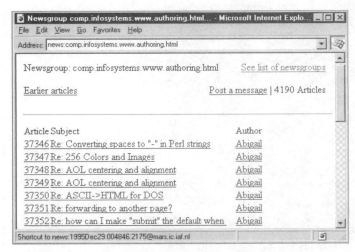

FIGURE 3-1: Usenet

BBSes

BBSes (see Figure 3-2) were the first type of social sites that enabled users to log on and interact with one another. The first BBSes came online in the late 70s. Originally these were primarily hosted on personal computers, and users had to dial in through the host computer's modem. Only one person at a time could gain access to the BBS.

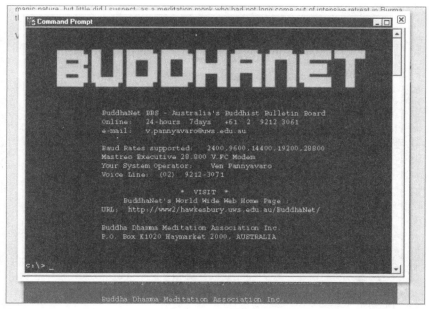

FIGURE 3-2: A BBS

Although there were legitimate BBSs, most were at least somewhat involved in illicit or illegal practices or included other questionable content such as adult material, virus code, and information and instructions for hacking and phreaking (phone hacking).

Online Services

After BBSes came online services such as CompuServe, AOL (see Figure 3-3), and Prodigy. These were the first real attempts to access the Internet using a service available to the general public. At the same time, they began to create a feel of a community around their users.

CompuServe was the first company to incorporate a chat program into its service. Prodigy was responsible for making online service more affordable. Genie was an early online service created by a General Electric subsidiary (GEIS) in 1985, and it was one of the earliest available services. It was a text-based service created to use idle time-sharing mainframes after normal business hours; it is considered the first viable commercial competition to CompuServe. Genie offered games, shopping, mail, and forums.

AOL started as an online service, too, and made great strides at making the Internet more universally accessible in the United States.

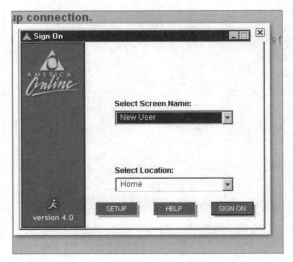

FIGURE 3-3: An early AOL login screen

IRC, ICQ, and Instant Messaging

Internet Relay Chat (IRC) was developed in 1988 and used for file sharing, link sharing, and keeping in touch. It was the father of instant messaging (IM) as we know it today. IRC was mostly UNIX-based, though, which limited access to most people.

ICQ (a pseudo-acronym for "I Seek You") was developed in the mid-'90s and was the first instant messaging program for PCs (see Figure 3-4). It was at least partly responsible for the adoption of avatars, abbreviations (such as LOL for "laugh out loud" and BRB for "be right back") and emoticons. Other IM clients soon followed.

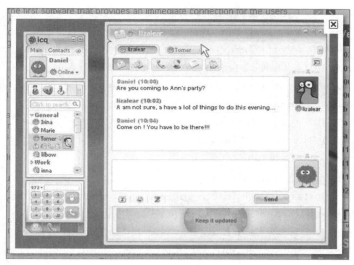

FIGURE 3-4: ICQ in use

Forums

An Internet *forum* is a discussion area on a website. These were descendents of the BBSes popular in the '70s and '80s, and played a large part in the evolution of the social web. Although they were originally based on the BBS concept, online forums came with a more user-friendly interface, making them easier for nontechnical visitors to use. Various forum platforms, including vBulletin and phpbb, were developed. Many of these are still used for forums. Forums remain a popular part of online culture, and many have made strides to add more social networking-type features.

An Internet forum is also referred to as a message board, discussion group, bulletin board, or web forum. These types of forums differ from an individual blog in one important way. A blog is most often written by one person, whereas an Internet forum typically enables its members to make posts and start new topics, so it is written by multiple people.

The Internet forum is not a real-time chat room. This is because with a chat room, people chat and communicate in real time; the members of an Internet forum post messages to be read by other members whenever they happen to log on.

> **?** Internet forums are usually focused on a single topic.

Before prospective members join an Internet forum and make posts to others, they are usually required to register. The prospective members must agree to follow the Terms of Service. These typically include such things as to respect other members and refrain from using profanity. When members are approved by the administrator or moderator of the Internet forum, the members usually choose their usernames and passwords. Sometimes, a password is supplied. An avatar or photograph can be uploaded by the members to appear under their username in each post or comment they make.

The different conversations in an Internet forum are called *threads*, which consist of posts written by the members. Members can typically edit their own posts, start new topics, post in their choice of threads, and edit their profile. A profile usually lists optional information about each forum member such as the city they are located in and their interests.

An Internet forum administrator or monitor may also participate in the forum. A forum administrator can modify threads and move or delete threads if necessary. There are also moderators who often help the administrator to moderate Internet forum members to make sure the forum rules are followed.

Dating Sites

Dating sites are sometimes considered the first social networks. The first dating sites cropped up almost as soon as people started going online. They enabled users to create profiles (usually with photos) and to contact other users. Although many people consider dating sites or sites like Classmates.com to be the first social networks, they don't actually fit the definition. Dating sites rarely enable you to keep a friends list—neither did Classmates in its early years (and profiles were severely limited). Because users could not serendipitously find and connect with people in an open forum, and therefore not share connections with others, the sites were actually inherently anti-social.

Six Degrees

Six Degrees (see Figure 3-5) was launched in 1997 and was the first modern social network. It enabled users to create a profile and to become friends with other users. Although the site no longer exists, at one time it was actually quite popular and had approximately one million members at its peak. In 2000, Six Degrees was purchased for $125 million.

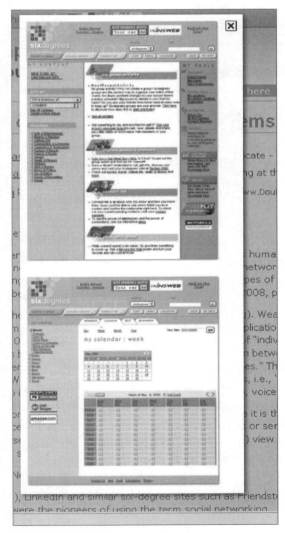

FIGURE 3-5: Six Degrees desktop

LiveJournal

LiveJournal (see Figure 3-6) started in 1999 and took a different approach to social networking. Six Degrees enabled users to create a basically static profile, whereas LiveJournal was a social network built around constantly updated blogs. LiveJournal encouraged its users to follow one another and to create groups and interact. It was the precursor to the live updates you currently see in social networks.

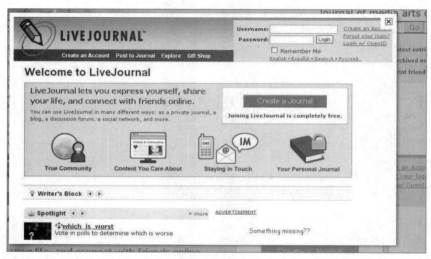

FIGURE 3-6: Welcome page for LiveJournal

Friendster

The dawn of the new century brought with it some huge developments in social networking and social media. Friendster was the first widely used social network of the 2000–2010 decade. Founded in 2002, Friendster was shut down on May 31, 2011. Prior to its closure, Friendster had more than 90 million registered users and 60+ million unique visitors each month. Almost 90 percent of Friendster traffic came from Asia.

Friendster built its interactions around enabling people to discover their friends and then friends-of-friends, and so on to expand their networks. The goal was to be a safer place to meet new people than in real life—and be faster.

At its core, Friendster acted like a dating service. Instead of matching complete strangers based on shared interests, it operated on the assumption that people with shared friends and acquaintances would have a better chance than those who had no shared connection.

Since the creation and subsequent overtake of services like MySpace and Facebook, Friendster evolved into a gaming site, with its primary demographic residing in Southeast Asia. In April 2011, the service announced it would delete all user data by May 31, 2011.

Hi5

Another early powerful social network was Hi5. It was launched in 2003 and currently has more than 60 million active members.

Profile privacy works a bit differently on Hi5, where a user's network consists of not only their own contacts, but also second-degree (friends of friends) and third-degree contacts (friends of friends of friends).

Users can set their profiles to be seen only by their network members or by Hi5 users in general. Although Hi5 is not particularly popular in the United States, it has a large user base in parts of Asia, Latin America, and Central Africa.

LinkedIn

LinkedIn was founded in 2003 and was one of the first mainstream social networks devoted to business. Originally, LinkedIn enabled users to post a profile (see Figure 3-7), which acted like a resume, and to interact through private messaging. It also works on the assumption that you should personally know the people you connect with on the site.

Gradually, other features have been added, including groups, question and answer forums, company pages and advanced profile features, including real-time updates.

LinkedIn has grown to become a way for users to connect based on professional experience and recommendations. As you connect with more people, your network grows and your opportunity to professionally connect with others you don't already know grows as well. The larger your LinkedIn network, the greater your possibility for meeting and connecting with anyone you may need to in your professional career.

FIGURE 3-7: LinkedIn profile

MySpace

Founded in 2003, MySpace became the biggest social network within three years. Its most popular feature, inciting a new generation of creative web services, enables its users to decorate and customize their profile pages. Its users can also post music from artists on MySpace and embed videos from other sites on their profiles.

MySpace also enabled communication through private messages, public comments posted to a user's profile, and bulletins sent out to all one's friends. In 2006, MySpace introduced MySpace IM, an instant messaging client that enables users to chat with their friends.

Facebook

It began as a Harvard-only social network in 2004 and quickly expanded to other schools and then to high schools, businesses, and the general public. In 2008, Facebook became the most popular social networking site, surpassing MySpace, and it continues to grow.

Facebook doesn't allow for the level of customization that MySpace does. It does, however, enable users to post photos, videos, and links (see Figure 3-8). Facebook has added a number of features over the past few years, including instant messaging and email addresses.

FIGURE 3-8: Facebook profile page

Users have a few different methods to communicate with one another. Private messaging is available and writing on another user's Wall. Users can easily change their privacy settings to allow different users to see different parts of their profile, based on the existing relationships. The default settings for privacy are "only me," "friends," "friends of friends," and "everyone." Facebook now allows filtering of friends using lists, so that different lists are able to see different content. If you don't want co-workers to see pictures that friends post on your wall, you can filter co-workers so that they can't view this type of content.

Users can also comment on or "Like" the posts of their friends, and conversations often occur within the comment sections among multiple people.

Ning

Ning is a platform for creating niche social networks. Networks are hosted by Ning but can take on their own personality and can even pay to have their own branding instead of the Ning brand.

New users can either create social networks for any niche they choose or join any of the more than 1.5 million existing networks.

Ning was the first widely used social networking platform. Its biggest advantage in the market was that it made it incredibly simple for even nontechnical users to set up their own social network.

Twitter

Twitter was founded in 2006 and gained a lot of popularity during the 2007 SXSW (South by Southwest) conference. Tweets tripled during the conference, from 20k per day to 60k. Twitter has developed a cult-like following and has a number of famous users such as Ashton Kutcher, President Barack Obama, Tiger Woods, and Oprah.

Next to Facebook, Twitter has had the most impact on the social networking sphere as a whole. With the launch of Twitter, status updates have become the new norm in social networking. Virtually all major social networks now enable real-time updates. Twitter is discussed later in the book.

Posterous

Posterous is a microblogging application, started in May 2009. Users post content via email. Emails can include attached photos, MP3s, and other file types that are also posted. No initial signup is needed, setting it apart from most other social media services.

Tumblr

Tumblr is sort of a cross between a life-streaming application and a microblogging platform. Tumblr was founded in 2007 and had approximately 75,000 Tumble bloggers start using the service pretty much immediately.

The service enables users to post photos, video, text, audio, links, conversations, and other content on these blog-like sites. There are mobile applications available for posting to Tumblr, making it ideal for lifestreaming.

Tumblr is also easy to use, making it well-suited to less technical users. It's similar to Twitter and other microblogging platforms in the way that it enables you follow other Tumblr users to see their updates in a specialized dashboard feed. Users can also "heart" (favorite) other Tumblr users' content and reblog posts from other users, keeping the original credit intact.

Tumblr's terms of service requires that users grant Tumblr a "non-exclusive, worldwide, royalty-free, transferable right and license (with the right to sublicense, to use, copy, cache, publish, display, distribute, modify, create derivative works and store" content). Make sure to read the Terms of Service on sites, especially if copyrights are essential to your content.

Rule of Thumb   If a site or service allows you to talk to others in an open way, where others can witness the communication, this site or service is social.

Related Questions

➜ 5. What is my brand's objective? **Page 18**

➜ 22. What can I install on my website to encourage conversations? **Page 75**

➜ 65. What is social bookmarking? **Page 181**

➜ 92. How should I describe the platforms I choose? **Page 249**

Action Item

➜ For every site on which you create a profile, note the web address to your profile. Create an icon or text link on your website and allow users to find your profiles on these networks through these web links.

Importance

13. How Do I Choose Which Sites to Use?

Lisa Barone, the co-founder and chief branding officer at Outspoken Media, created six questions to ask yourself when deciding which social network is right for you. Each of these questions is discussed in the following sections.

Determine the Strengths of the Site

Whether it's Twitter, DailyBooth, or Flickr, it doesn't matter: Before you decide to allocate resources to a particular site, know why you are joining it. How will being on Twitter help your business? What can you do on this site more efficiently than through a different network? What is your goal of being on this network? Unless you want to get smacked, don't just recite what you read on Mashable or some other social media blog. Actually evaluate the site and decide how its functionality can help your brand's critical success factors. Just because LinkedIn is great for one business does not mean it is going to be a fit for your business. You need to find what is. Social media is about having an opportunity to promote your brand and position it as an industry (or local) leader. Decide what you need and how this site can help you get it. If you can't figure out how this site will help you, find another one.

Determine the Time You Can Afford to Spend on It

When evaluating the time you can spend on a social network site, be realistic. How much time can you realistically spend to maintain your Facebook page? An hour a day? An hour a week? An hour a month?

The amount of time you can spend will be directly tied to whether you're successful. Scott Stratten often states in presentations that his Twitter followers really started to grow when he began dedicating a significant amount of time to interacting on Twitter. (At the time of writing this chapter, Scott had 74,768 followers.) Shocking, right? Well, not really. These are social channels. To see a return on them, you have to actually be social on them. If you have only half an hour a week to build brand awareness, it's probably not going to work for you. Social media, much like SEO and most other parts of your marketing identify, are not one-time investments. You need to actually be there and show people that you're part of that community. The only thing worse than not having a presence on an important social network is having a crappy one because then it's not ignorance, it's just that you don't care. If you don't have time to raise the baby, don't have one. It means less therapy for everyone.

> **Rule of Thumb** Even if you don't have content to post, you should go on the networks to see what people are talking about and if anyone is trying to have a conversation with you. Social networks are not about what you have to say, but instead are about with whom you converse.

Determine the Demands of the Site

When you create that social media account, you're actually expected to do something with it. If it's a Twitter account, you need someone to update, respond to comments, and generally communicate with other people. If it's YouTube, you are responsible for creating video, promoting it, and being active in that community. If it's a DailyBooth account, well, you'll have to find someone who is vain enough to take photos of himself on a regular basis. All these sites demand that your brand participate in some way. Make sure you understand what those demands are before you get on the bandwagon. If you have no social skills, don't join.

Determine Your Community Social Network Needs

Even if you think they are, have you checked to see that your target market uses the social network you plan to use? Just because the world now spends 110 billion minutes (OMG, go outside!) on social networks and blogs, that doesn't mean your users do. Check your referrals to see where your community is hanging out and where your content already is. Go to the social network you're courting and do a search for your brand and keywords. Are conversations taking place there? Do a search for your competitors. Are people having conversations with or about them? Ask your customers about the social networks they most use (if any) and if they'd like to see you there. Don't just assume that your audience is on Twitter or Facebook because they're the most popular. You want to have the numbers in your hand to back up whatever site you choose.

Determine the Costs and Affordability

Really, would you join if it cost you to do so? If the only reason you're signing up with this social network is because you think it's free, don't join. Although the site may not charge for membership, you pay for presence there. You pay in your time and the resources that you dedicate to it. If this site isn't important enough to you that you'd pay to be a member, it's a sign you're not taking it seriously. Don't waste your time or anyone else's.

Determine Integration Capabilities

You learned about the difference between creating a social media campaign and a social media strategy. The latter is what produces the best results. Doing social media "on purpose" as opposed to just falling into it means integrating one site's activity with everything else you do. How can your social media presence on this site integrate with what you do offline? How can it become part of your email marketing? How can it work into day-to-day customer interactions? People and departments fail when you restrict them to an island. Every time you set up a new port, you need to create a bridge.

Obviously, you won't know 100 percent whether a site will work for you until you test the waters and start connecting with other people. But by answering the previous questions, it can help you hone in on the sites that can give your brand the biggest boost. Social media success begins with picking the right home.

Developing an Online Community

An online community, or a virtual community, is a network of individuals who interact through specific media, potentially crossing geographical and political boundaries to pursue mutual interests or goals. One of the most pervasive types of an online community includes social networking services, which consist of various online communities.

These online communities encourage interaction, sometimes focusing around a particular interest, or sometimes just to communicate. Quality virtual communities do both. They enable users to interact over a shared passion, whether it is through message boards, chat rooms, social networking sites, or virtual worlds.

 Related Questions

➜ 14. Why do I need to be selective?   **Page 56**

➜ 64. What sites can help me find relevant news?   **Page 176**

➜ 74. What brand monitoring tools can I use?   **Page 204**

➜ 92. How should I describe the platforms I choose?   **Page 249**

Action Item

➜ Create a spreadsheet of all the different features that are important to you, cross-referenced with the sites you are considering using. This will help to narrow your choices with data.

Importance

14. Why Do I Need to Be Selective?

Although it is important to protect your brand by creating a username on your relevant networking sites, it can be just as important to be selective about which sites you actually use for your brand. There are so many networks to choose from, and establishing a username at any and all of them is not a bad idea. This can prevent others from taking the username and possibly confusing consumers with conflicting brand names.

However, putting 20 different icons that link to your 20 different online profiles can be just as confusing and damaging to your brand as having a conflicting one.

As a social media strategist, there are many different sites on which I can choose to establish a presence: Twitter, Facebook, Friendfeed, Mashable Follow, LinkedIn, Digg, Reddit, FourSquare... the list does go on and on. However, all of these sites can cause people who want to follow online to be overwhelmed.

Before selecting the sites on which to take an active presence, it's important to determine what each site will do (both positively and negatively) for your brand. Some things to consider when making the decision:

Determine Why You Like a Site

Did a popular tech blog article convince you that the network was the best thing since sliced bread? Have you looked at it and enjoyed the way people communicate on it? Are you not entirely sure, and want to just check it out? Sign up for a username. Just because you have a username doesn't mean you have to use the site. In some cases, having a username on a site even if it remains inactive can be positive simply because it supports your effort to be consistent across all online platforms. If someone else grabbed your username before you, it could be more damaging than having an inactive account.

Determine Where Your Customers Are

Do a lot of your clients use Twitter? Does Meetup.com play a big part in your industry? Are you a location that a lot of people like to check into on Foursquare? Pay attention to where your business is coming from, and where your customers are when they're doing activities unrelated to your business. If you have a huge fan base among college students, you may want to go on the networks that interest them (like Facebook) rather than LinkedIn, where none of them would have yet established a profile.

Rule of Thumb   Make social sites work for you by maximizing your presence on the sites that your target market utilizes. These will be the easiest sites for people who already are qualified to support your brand to find you, and will result in less work in the development of a community foundation.

Determine How You Are Going to Use the Site

If you intend to use Twitter for business and Facebook for personal reasons, don't use the same username. You're actually making two separate efforts for two separate brands, and you shouldn't confuse the two or you will confuse your consumers. Decide how you want to use each network now because what you write on those networks will be accessible for pretty much forever, and you don't want to leave the wrong impression.

Determine What You Can Automate

If you are absolutely determined to use Delicious to socially bookmark interesting sites, establish a profile on the site. There are plug-ins or extensions that you can add to your web browser that will make saving your bookmarks a one-step process rather than requiring you to go to the site and save them manually. As a blogger, it may prove useful to automatically append your feed to networks so that your RSS feed updates sites like Facebook, Alltop, LinkedIn, and others automatically with content.

Related Questions

→ 5. What is my brand's objective? **Page 18**

→ 12 What social networks best fit my goals? **Page 40**

→ 93. What metrics should I use to gauge my return on investment? **Page 250**

→ 99. How do I keep from being overwhelmed? **Page 263**

Action Item

→ Review your existing social presence. Deactivate or delete any profile on a site that might have a negative impact on your brand.

Creating a Website

In this chapter:

Importance

15. How Do I Set Up a Website?

Setting up a website can take as little as 20 minutes. The most important parts of the process are selecting a domain name (the website address) and choosing a hosting plan (deciding how much space your website hosting provider needs to allocate to your website).

There are many website hosting providers available to use. Deciding which one to use will be based on your budget and your space needs. As a general rule, the more media your website requires (video, audio, images) the more space your website will need.

Some website hosting providers offer free hosting in exchange for ad placement on your site. Depending on your needs, this may be a great option for the brands with lower budgets.

Website hosting providers will guide you through the process of purchasing hosting space. When you're done, you'll have your account all set up but you still won't necessarily have a website.

To fully set it up, you must take note of certain information. File Transfer Protocol (FTP) settings are used to connect your offline files to your online space. You will need these settings, which are obtainable after you purchase your hosting package, to either upload files yourself to set up the site or to give to your website developer.

There are quicker ways to set up a website. Most website hosting providers include a library of programs that can be easily installed with the click of a button. Platforms like WordPress can be set up in a matter of minutes, and act like a "website in a box" (see Figure 4-1).

Setting up a website in WordPress offers many great options. If you are unsure about your content and how to make revisions to it later when first setting up your website, WordPress can offer an easy way to manage the content on your website with little to no website creation experience. Two different WordPress sites are available: http://wordpress.com/ that hosts free websites and http://wordpress.org/ that holds the files you need to place on your hosting server to manage the hosting on your own.

FIGURE 4-1: An example of a free site built on Wordpress

Picking between hosting your own WordPress site and having it hosted for free elsewhere will largely depend on how much control you want over the site. If you want to be able to customize the design and site functionality so that it's unique to your business, you will need to host your own site. If you are more concerned with getting content developed and having a presence online without too much concern about custom design or functionality, a site on `WordPress.com` works fine.

Related Questions

➜ 5. What is my brand's objective? **Page 18**

➜ 10. How do I brand my online identity? **Page 34**

➜ 22. What can I install on my website to encourage conversations? **Page 75**

➜ 23. How do I add a blog to my website? **Page 82**

Action Item

➜ Review hosting options from providers like Dreamhost, GoDaddy, or Fatcow and compare pricing for your website services.

Importance

16. What Should I Use as My Website Address?

Before you rush out and choose your domain name or name your website, keep in mind that your domain name should be your website name as well. This can be difficult because domain names can often be hard to come by.

Naming a site after its domain name is important, for the simple reason that when people think of your website, they'll think of it by name. If your name is also your URL, they'll automatically know where to go. For example, when people think of chevys.com, they don't have to wonder what URL to type into their browser to get there. The name of the site is also the URL.

Imagine if your business (or website) is called Mount Carmel, but somebody else holds that domain name. Instead, you have some obscure domain name called, say, ilike-mountcarmel.com. What happens when your customers, recalling that Mount Carmel is a place they want to go, type www.mountcarmel? They'll end up at the wrong place and may stay there.

What if you cannot get the domain name of your choice? What you do depends on how committed you are to that particular name. If you have an existing brand name that you're known for, you'll probably not want to eliminate that name just because you couldn't get the domain name. After all, it took you a lot of time and money to establish that name. If so, you might simply want to try to buy the domain name from the current owner. You can find information about current owners by checking out a site like whois.net (see Figure 4-2).

On the other hand, if you're just starting out, you might prefer the cheaper alternative of trying to obtain a domain name first, and then naming your website (or self-brand) after the domain that you've acquired. So if you've acquired the domain name thedavepeck, your website and brand might be named thedavepeck or thedavepeck.com. I know this seems a bit like putting the cart before the horse, but that's the reality if you don't want to lose out on your website name.

A domain name that matches your brand name is important. The name that you use to advertise your product is the name that you want for your domain because that is the first thing that people will try in their browser. It is also the easiest thing for them to remember, and

Can't get the domain you want? Try adding "The" or "My" to the front of it. Hey, it works for me...

A domain name system, or DNS, is like a phone number; it gives every Internet website an easy to remember name. They then mask the DNS number. Examples are donateportal.com, popchips.com, and antoniosabatojronline.com.

whatever is easily remembered will be more likely to be tried out than an obscure domain name.

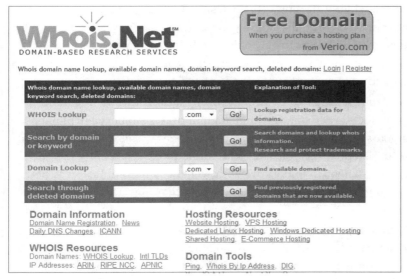

FIGURE 4-2: The whois.net website

Related Questions

+ 7. Am I reflecting my brand? **Page 22**
+ 10. How do I brand my online identity? **Page 34**
+ 11. Why does an email address matter? **Page 36**
+ 15. How do I set up a website? **Page 60**

Action Items

+ Make a list of your top five website address choices and see if you can get them. Check out the who.is information for the sites you cannot purchase outright.

+ Check out the `whois.net` information for the domain, and contact the person listed to see if he or she is willing to sell it. You probably should be aware that the current owner is likely to charge a higher fee than you'll normally get when buying new domains (assuming that the owner is willing to sell it).

Importance

17. How Do I Design My Website?

As you consider different website design options, you must be clear about your website goals. When you know what you want to say and what you want visitors to do, you're ready to create your website. With your goals in mind, you can navigate the field of web design by focusing on what kind of content you intend to have.

Are you looking to only provide information on your website, or is there some interactivity and engagement that is supposed to happen? Your goals for your site will greatly direct the type of website you need to build. Establishing yourself as an industry expert will likely mean that you will need to make sure your website is content heavy. Whether it be through text or images, your site should be designed with content in mind.

If your goal is to provide an online avenue for communicating with your company, then your site will be much smaller because the website is used to entice interest only rather than be a fully informative site that keeps people coming back for more education about your business. Websites like these are called "brochure sites" and essentially act as an electronic version of a business flier or brochure (hence the name).

The content on your website will also drive the design. Once you've figured out the content, you'll be able to build your navigation on top of that. Then, you can determine how much will be images and how much will be text, what will go in the main content area, and what may go in the sidebar or footer. An online lingerie store will have a different look and feel than a photographer's portfolio, a church site, a real-estate company, or a sports team site. You'll also now be able to decide what types of content will be added to drive people to your social sites.

Rule of Thumb   Brochure sites typically make use of icons that lead to social profiles, where content-rich sites will usually use more inclusive social integration, like a feed of your most recent Twitter or Facebook content.

Pre-designed website templates can help you create a website even if you don't have design skills, time, or a huge budget. Most templates allow you to make changes in order to reflect your existing brand. Customization ranges from color and font selection and adding your company logo all the way to adding multimedia and flash animation. Make sure the template you choose to create a website will support the degree of customization that you require.

Related Questions

➧ 2. Brand, Online Presence—What's the difference? **Page 4**

➧ 7. Am I reflecting my brand? **Page 22**

➧ 10. How do I brand my online identity? **Page 34**

➧ 18. Is a logo important? **Page 66**

Action Item

➧ Look at your major competitors and see what type of content they have on their websites. This will help you figure out a path for your own website and can help you figure out what you do or do not like about certain design features.

Importance

18. Is a Logo Important?

Logos can be either graphic or text-based, or a combination of both. Although many consider logos important in terms of being recognizable, the more important idea is that our brand is recognizable, period. If you feel that your brand can make a greater impact and impression by creating a graphic to represent it, then the answer to this question would be "absolutely yes." Some brands that rely on solo graphics to represent them include Target, McDonalds, or Starbucks.

If the name of your brand is already one that stands out or makes an impact, then a graphical logo becomes less important. Some brands that are great examples of this are *The New York Times*, Gap, Sprite, and Mashable. In other situations, a combined graphic and text logo makes sense. Some brands can achieve this by using unique fonts, such as Facebook, Twitter, or Virgin Airlines.

On social networking websites, because the use of an avatar is available, using a business name for a username can be sufficient. The avatar, or image to represent the account, should be reserved for an actual person's image. This gives the social network profile personality and other people will feel like they are communicating, interacting, and engaging with actual people.

On a website, the use of a logo (graphic, textual, or both) can be important because it truly represents the overall brand. For a 30-person business, one person's image on the brand's Twitter account is fine because that person represents the entire brand. On a website, the logo will represent the entire brand rather than just putting that responsibility on a person. In general, the thing to remember is that websites are meant for people to find more information about your brand in the professional sense. On a social network, people are trying to connect with the personal side of your brand and need to engage with a real person instead of a logo.

Related Questions

Action Item

➔ Sketch five different logo ideas and allow no more than two trusted friends help you decide which idea best reflects your brand.

Importance

19. What Pages Are Essential for My Website?

The possibilities are endless for the types of pages you can have on a website. A website needs several "core" pages. Darren Rowse of Pro-Blogger states that there approximately 20 different pages you should consider when creating a site. Actually, you can break your website into four minimum types of pages. As defined by ProBlogger, they are:

- About page
- Contact page
- FAQ page
- Home page

About Page

The About page is considered the most important page of your site. Having an About page is essential because it gives new readers to your blog a snapshot of who you are and why they should subscribe to your blog. This is the page that I go to every time I hit a new blog. If one doesn't exist, it significantly decreases my chances of subscribing. Your About page should consist of the following:

- **Photo**—A picture of you is best.
- **Site objectives**—What is it about? What will readers gain from it?
- **Introduction of yourself**—Talk about your experience with the topic you're writing about. Why should they listen to you? What is your context and background?

Contact Page

Your Contact page needs to consist of the different ways a reader of your site can reach out to you. It should include the following:

- Your email address
- Social networking sites you can be found on
- Your mailing address

If you do not want to put your email address on the Web, you can create an email address that you use only for the website, something such as support@yourwebsitename.com.

FAQ Page

FAQ stands for Frequently Asked Questions. They are an important part of a website, and many people view an FAQ page as a huge timesaver when trying to find information. This is the place to drop answers to the questions you get all the time. Those commonly asked questions might be:

- How did you get started?
- How can I get in touch with you? (for those people who cannot locate your contact page)
- Do you speak at events?
- Where can I buy your product?

Home Page

This page is your landing page. This is the first page people see when they visit your site. This is where your most current blog post, your current content, or latest update appears. Your site's home page is often the first contact that visitors have with your site. A good home page helps turn casual visitors into repeat visitors. Following are some key things to keep in mind when creating and updating your home page:

- **Bulleted items**—People often scan these first and ignore text in paragraph form, so include your most important points in bullet lists. You can even create custom bullets for more emphasis.
- **Clearly defined sections**—Use color, header tags, or horizontal rules to structure your page into sections.
- **Columns**—These are easier to scan than long lines of text that spread across the whole page.
- **Short paragraphs**—Make your major point early in the paragraph because people often won't read the entire text. Use these techniques to briefly describe what you offer and explain why it's valuable. Then provide links so that visitors who want more

information can go deeper into the site. Your home page is the appetizer that makes visitors hungry for more.

➤ **Quick links**—If you have a mailing list or social profile links, placing them in noticeable sections on your home page will help bring focus to these links and increase the likelihood that people will use them.

Additional Content

Depending on your product or service, additional content may be needed to fully provide visitors with everything they need from your site. Plug-ins offer added functionality in pre-packaged code for website owners to include this additional content without a lot of financial investment. Some plug-ins, like Akismet, combat spam whereas others makes it easier for visitors to share your content with others using Facebook, Twitter, or StumbleUpon. The WordPress plug-in WP-Robot pulls in content from all over the Internet such as Amazon reviews, articles from news pages, and videos from YouTube.

You do not need plugins to succeed in blogging, but they can make your life easier. Imagine manually emailing any new posts that are put on your blog to your subscribers. That would take you hours, right? Well, you can get a plug-in to do this for you with little to no ongoing effort from you. With a plug-in, you can even automatically send out a Tweet every time your blog is updated.

 Related Questions

➤ 5. What is my brand's objective? **Page 18**

➤ 15. How do I set up a website? **Page 60**

➤ 17. How do I design my website? **Page 64**

➤ 38. What should I do if I don't want a blog? **Page 110**

Action Item

➤ Create an organizational chart using PowerPoint or a similar program and start creating your navigational page structure for the pages you want on your site and in what hierarchy.

20. Would Collecting Email Addresses Be Worthwhile?

Importance

Collecting email addresses can be a tricky thing. Many people are protective of their email addresses because they want to prevent possible issues with spam or unsolicited mail. Other people are afraid that releasing email addresses may cause potential privacy issues.

Before collecting email addresses, you have to consider how you will use the information. If you're using it for email marketing campaigns, make sure that those email-marketing campaigns will have a purpose and you're not just trying to communicate once in a while news about your company. That's better achieved through a news section or blog. An email marketing campaign that has targeted goals and tips with useful information for consumers will be a better use of email data.

If you need email addresses to communicate upcoming releases of beta or other versions of your software, it may be useful to have this data so that you can qualify potential users. Maintaining a database of interested people can help you to gauge the interest in your product or service.

If the email address' sole purpose is to validate a user based on confirmation (to reduce spam and unqualified visits), consider making this process social instead. Facebook and Twitter both use an open "graph" that allows users to input their Facebook or Twitter usernames and data to verify their identity. Your site doesn't store their passwords or usernames, and you qualify users before they can log in or apply to your program. You also have an added benefit of increasing your Facebook or Twitter fan base if you utilize these connectivity options.

If you're not sure whether or not you want to have an email newsletter, here are some reasons why you may consider it. If you don't find that you identify with any of the reasons below, you probably don't need to have an email newsletter.

+ A newsletter keeps your brand fresh in the minds of your customers. By sending a newsletter regularly, it offers the opportunity for you to keep your subscribers informed.

+ Establish yourself as a trusted expert. People search online for information and will look to you, as a subject matter expert, to provide it to them. Every week (or whatever schedule works) provides an opportunity to build on this, while reinforcing your brand.

➔ Build a relationship with the people on your list. It's common knowledge that people like to buy from people they like. By using newsletters to connect with readers, you can develop a relationship of familiarity and trust. Be sure to share a little about yourself or your company in every issue, whether it is an anecdote, event, or employee spotlight.

➔ Drive traffic to your website or blog. Remember to call attention to new blog posts or other changes to your website with links directly to those pages. Remind readers of your online newsletter archives.

➔ Build content on your website. Make a habit to add your electronic magazines and newsletters to your website in an archive area. This serves several important purposes:

  ➔ If you optimize your article placements, you will not only make your website "meatier," but you'll also bring new traffic from the search engines.

  ➔ Get feedback from your readers. Make it easy for you to stay in touch with prospects and customers and vice versa. Ask them to take action and comment on your articles and offers. Conduct polls and surveys. Start a "Letters to the Editor" column in your newsletter. Feedback allows you to fine tune your messages, target your marketing, and expand your product line. It's also great for relationship building!

  ➔ Grow your mailing list. Let your subscribers work for you. Be sure to remind your readers that it's okay to forward your newsletter to anyone they'd like. In addition, it's important to include sign-up instructions for those who received your ezine from viral marketing methods.

  ➔ Gather demographic data. By offering surveys, feedback forms, and niche reports, you'll be able to get valuable information about your prospects and customers. Learn what makes your readers tick, how to better serve them, and how to give them what they want.

The bottom line is that collecting email addresses is worthwhile only if the information distributed to user email addresses will be considered worthwhile to them. If your plan is to just use email as another avenue to feed information about your company rather than to grow and improve communication with your brand, then collecting email addresses would not be worthwhile. If your brand has a solid, stated plan to utilize the email addresses in something worthwhile to the consumer, then collecting them would be worthwhile to you.

> If you do decide to collect email addresses, make sure that you create a page on your website that details your privacy policy. The privacy policy lets people understand how you intend to use data.

 Related Questions

- ➜ 6. Who is my target audience? **Page 20**
- ➜ 22. What can I install on my website to encourage conversations? **Page 75**

Action Item

- ➜ Go to your email program and make sure your contacts are saved and contain complete information. This will be handy later.

Importance

21. Should I Have Ads on My Website?

Again, the answer to that question is another question (or two). If you put ads on your site, what would be their purpose and would they have a positive impact on your brand? If you have ads on your website because you are using a free service, you may actually be causing damage to your brand. By using a free service, you might potentially show consumers that you don't want to invest in yourself, which might make them question whether or not to invest in you.

If the ads are there because you are a blogger, and the advertisers are supporters and sponsors of the website from which you make your living, readers will likely understand that because your content is free to them, and the advertisers will help to ensure that they continue to receive valuable content at no cost.

Websites that promote particular products might also consider advertising that supports the brand. For example, a fitness studio website might contain advertisements for nutritional supplements. This showcases a strategic partnership that supports the fitness studio's role as a knowledgeable industry participant. On the other hand, a web design studio advertising free website templates might be contradicting the brand expertise while drawing people away from the website.

When considering advertisements, the main thing to remember is that the advertisements (like collecting email addresses) should have a purpose that cannot be misconstrued by the public as inappropriate or damaging to the brand.

Advertisement placement services can filter content so that the ads used are not contradictory to the brand. For example, the web design studio could specify keywords that should be avoided when ads are rotated in.

 Related Questions

- ➤ 5. What is my brand's objective? **Page 18**
- ➤ 7. Am I reflecting my brand? **Page 22**

Action Item

- ➤ Take a look at your existing traffic if you have a site. Use the tools on Google Ads to determine the rate per click you would get...is it worth it?

22. What Can I Install on My Website to Encourage Conversations?

Importance

There are many different plug-ins and codes that can be included on a website to encourage conversations. The codes or plug-ins to use will vary depending on your purpose and intended usage on the site.

Social Plugins

The most commonly used plug-ins are the ones let you add the content to Facebook, Twitter, LinkedIn, or other services immediately from the website or article. Commonly referred to as the Like button (Facebook), the Tweet button (Twitter), Digg button, or +1 (Google), these plug-ins are often used on blogs to promote social sharing. Nearly every social network has a button that you can install on your website to encourage conversation. The social networks will also have instructions for how to install, including giving you the code directly and allowing you to essentially just copy and paste it over into your website. Sites based in WordPress, Joomla, Drupal, or other similar content management systems often can take advantage of ready-made code that can be installed with a simple upload.

Comment Systems

The most commonly used plug-ins are the ones let you integrate comments into commenter's social networks. Disqus is a blog-commenting system, an external service used in blogs to offer a versatile, yet easy-to-use platform for both the readers and the bloggers to make blog commenting a better experience for everyone.

Disqus integrates to all major blogging platforms, including some free, hosted platforms, such as Tumblr.com and Blogger, and self-hosted CMS systems such as WordPress, Drupal, and Joomla, just to name the most popular ones. It offers a chance to moderate comments on a blog via an external service, and a place for the blog commenters to track and manage their own comments with ease.

Disqus consists of two parts: one is for the bloggers and the other is for the blog readers, or the blog commenters actually. The comment and moderation system for bloggers is the Disqus Comments. The blog comment aggregation and social profile for a blog commenter is called Disqus Profile.

Disqus Comments, like most free services, it is far from perfect. Disqus has some decent perks, which has made it a favorite for many bloggers. In combination with the single-login, auto sharing to Twitter and Facebook, and claiming and editing one's own comments with a Disqus Profile, Disqus is a powerful combination, which can benefit both the blogger(s) and the commenters.

Disqus is the quickest and easiest way to get a solid blog commenting system. Without Disqus, you're depending on the blogging platform, theme/template designer, addons/plugins, and your or someone else's technical knowledge to configure them all and get all the pieces in place and working.

Disqus is amazing for blog commenters. The single login (login once and never enter name, email, and URL for blog comments again), automatic sharing and replying to Twitter, and all the good stuff made me fall in love with Disqus as a blog commenter. As a result, I wanted my readers to get those cool benefits as well.

Really Simple Syndication (RSS) and Feeds

Getting information that is one of the keys to having an online presence. Knowing what is going on, who the influencers are, what your competition is doing, and breaking news. Going to a website every day or even every hour to see if there is an update can be a big time-management problem.

The RSS feed solves this problem and brings the updates to you. RSS is about getting live web feeds directly to your computer. RSS takes the latest headlines from different web sites and pushes those headlines down to your computer for quick scanning. The acronym RSS stands for many versions of the same thing.

- ✦ Really Simple Syndication
- ✦ Rich Site Summary

➤ RDF Site Summary

➤ Real-time Simple Syndication

The four acronyms are all the same. They allow you to have web sites of your choice deliver their latest news directly to your computer. So instead of having to visit 14 different places to get your weather, sports, favorite photos, latest gossip, or latest political debates, you just go to one screen and see it combined or, as they say, aggregated into a single place. Once published at the source server, RSS headlines take only moments to bring it to your computer or reader.

Behind the scenes RSS headlines are simple text files that the publishing web master submits to a special feed server. That RSS feed server, in turn, pushes the text file to the screens of its subscribers. Time lag is usually 30 seconds to 30 minutes before the subscribers see the updates. In most cases, the lag is not even noticeable.

To get started using a RSS, you need an RSS reader tool for yourself. Most RSS readers are free to use and easy to learn. Set up your reader by loading the RSS feeds into your reader tool. This is achieved through multiple different ways. You can visit the web feed site directly, you can copy and paste the special code from an email, or you can load copies from your friend's RSS reader screen.

Then all you will need to do is simply log in to your RSS reader page or start your RSS software, and you can scan all your web feeds instantly. You can arrange the RSS feeds into folders just like email and you can even set alerts and sounds for when a particular web feed is updated.

Once you master the RSS, you want to move on to a slick enhancement for it called FeedBurner, which was purchased by Google. FeedBurner is a great way to track the number of visits you have to your blog and the number of subscribers your blog has, and it allows you to offer feed updates via email. In addition, FeedBurner can:

➤ Tell you if people who subscribe to your RSS are finding you interesting and engaging. Foremost, it introduces you to an interesting feature that analyzes the demand for your feed. When logging into FeedBurner, one of the first screens you will notice is the Feed Stats Dashboard. The dashboard provides various details about visitors' interactions with the feed. Here, it gives you a breakdown of your subscribers, how they subscribed, views, clicks, and more. Of course, try not to spend an immense amount of time analyzing these stats and focus your attention on increasing your subscriber count.

➤ Maybe your brand has a mix of loyal Twitter followers who do not subscribe to your RSS feed. Ideally, you want to reach out to these people. FeedBurner easily integrates with Twitter and in doing so it perpetually tweets your latest blog articles for you.

➤ When you visit Twitter, you might have noticed many short and strange URLs. These are called short URLs and are favorable for Twitter because each tweet is limited to 140 characters. Google has its own short URL service and when using FeedBurner, they are created automatically. This is another time-saving feature thanks to FeedBurner.

➤ Flickr is used by millions to manage and showcase photographs, digital art, website design portfolios, and much more. The advantage of using Flickr is that the images will invite traffic to your site. Images uploaded to Flickr can appear on your site as your photo gallery, but that's a different story. FeedBurner's Photo Splicer can connect to your Flickr Photostream and automatically add them to your RSS Feed. Your subscribers and Twitter followers will automatically be notified when photos have been uploaded. When first starting Flickr, you might have to promote its existence and this is one way to accomplish the task at hand.

➤ Because your father might say, "What the heck is an RSS feed?" the option to subscribe through email is available. Then there are many other readers available. After getting accustomed to RSS feeds, you might notice how many applications you currently use have a reader built into it. For instance, the newer version of Microsoft Outlook is one of them.

Related Questions

→ 23. How do I add a blog to my website? **Page 82**

→ 35. What is a blogroll? **Page 105**

→ 41. How do I increase my Twitter following? **Page 117**

→ 49. How do I get people to like my Facebook Page? **Page 143**

Action Item

→ If you have a WordPress blog, install Disqus and set up your profile.

Chapter 5
Making a Website Social

Importance

23. How Do I Add a Blog to My Website?

There are various ways that a blog can be added to a website. It can be either combined directly with your website to provide seamless transitioning for website visitors or it can be placed on one of the many free services available and you can redirect people to it using a navigation button on your website.

Blog feeds can also be added to a website by placing the most recent content on a page or within a sidebar. Then, when people click on the particular article headline, they can be redirected to your blog and led straight to the desired content.

The most common way to add a blog to a website is to utilize one of the many free platforms available. Wordpress is a popular tool that can be downloaded at www.wordpress.org and added straight to your website hosting. You can also set up an account at an external service like Tumblr or Posterous, and link your website to the separated blog.

> Blogger.com and Wordpress.com provide free hosting services on their own platforms for people to use. They even provide the option to purchase a personalized domain name while using their hosting.

 Rule of Thumb   A blog installed directly within a website is usually the preferred option for websites that rely heavily on SEO.

Related Questions

- ➤ 15. How do I set up a website? **Page 60**
- ➤ 19. What pages are essential for my website? **Page 68**
- ➤ 22. What can I install on my website to encourage conversations? **Page 75**
- ➤ 38. What should I do if I don't want a blog? **Page 110**

Action Items

- ➤ Choose one blog that you respect and enjoy reading. Place a link on your website to it.
- ➤ Follow up with a comment about liking the site or an email if you already connected with it.

24. What Do I Write About?

Importance

Getting inspired to write about something can be one the hardest things to do (see Figure 5-1). Sometimes you have to be in the right mood and right place to let that blog post come out. You can create a new post in several ways. The inspiration for these posts might come by responding to something elsewhere on the Web. The best way to start blogging is to simply link to something elsewhere that you feel is interesting or maybe something that you disagree with. If you make a constructive criticism to what someone else has posted, you can start a useful dialogue.

FIGURE 5-1: Where blogging inspiration comes from

In this response post, you can add links and endorse your point of view and stance.

When creating a post, present an idea for a different way to do things. Then invite people to present their reactions and suggestions to it. You cannot expect people to come to you. Taking it a step further, you should reach out to people you would not normally reach out to. A good post with an insightful look at something can drive a lot of traffic and keep readers coming back.

A hyperlink is a graphic or a piece of text in an Internet document that can connect readers to another web page or another portion of a document. Web users can usually find at least one hyperlink on every web page. The simple form of these is called embedded text or an embedded link.

A way to create a post is to conduct an interview. This is one of the most straightforward and easy ways to create a post. An email interview can work well, but if you can put an audio or video recording on the site, you will add value. If you interview busy people, limit your questions, or if you ask for their advice, specifically ask for their "three tips on...." or "five things I know about...." You can even turn this into a series of interviews with the same theme.

Another great way to develop content is to write live blog posts. Live blog from an event people might find interesting. Find a relevant event, conference, meeting, public talk, or demonstration and write your post while you're at the event. Start your post when the event begins and post up-to-the-minute quotes, announcements, comments, and insight.

Other types of post involves asking questions. This type of post works best after you have an established readership. When your readers know your style, stance, and feel, they know you and are more likely to leave comments. If there is a big piece of news in your industry, such as an acquisition or new product launch, ask your audience how it feels about it. Asking questions like these can help to draw insightful commentary from your readership.

You can also try to look for a fight. This tactic may not be the best, nor is it for those who are not thick-skinned. Yet, many bloggers attempt to generate traffic by loudly criticizing another popular blogger in the hope that the blogger will respond and generate traffic from his or her readers. This tactic is often referred to as *link-baiting*. In other words, if the criticized blogger responds (takes the bait), it generally means people will create links to your blog. If you criticize another blogger, then it is worth considering if it will be seen as link-bait or a constructive and valuable debate. Done well, a genuine argument between two bloggers can generate insight and bring factions to compromise. Try picking a fight with a company or brand and mount a campaign to instigate change.

You can also do something visual. You can take photographs or video footage as you travel along a particular route, for example. Explain them, ask questions, and include relevant links. Or, draw sketches and photograph them.

Live blogging is a great way to do up-to-the-minute reporting on an event. This is recommended only if there is a lot of traffic that's already coming to your website. If there's not a lot of traffic, a post event recap would suffice and be a lot less work.

Review something, such as a product or service that relates to your industry. Then try to make it useful by including links to it to receive feedback from other reviewers.

Lists are also enormously popular on the Web because people like lists. Lists can be one of the most effective ways to create a post. They are always shared and passed on. Some examples are "Top Ten Smoothie Kings" or "25 things to see in El Dorado Hills, California."

Tutorials also frequently top a website's most shared lists and can be enormously useful in generating goodwill in your sphere by attracting comments that then add to and improve your knowledge of a subject.

Finally, create a guest post. If you know people with particular expertise or experience, invite them to write a *guest post* on a particular subject. Even if they have their own blogs, they will probably appreciate the opportunity to reach a new audience, or to write in a different context, and again it can improve your own knowledge.

 Related Questions

➤ 34. Should I "guest blog?" **Page 102**

➤ 42. What should I tweet about? **Page 120**

➤ 69. What keywords do I use? **Page 193**

➤ 97. How can I build influence? **Page 258**

Action Item

➤ Take some time to browse websites and news items that are related to what you want to write about. Make a list of five topics you find interesting. From there get it down to one, and then write your first post.

Importance

25. What Tone Should I Use?

As a niche blogger, you are definitely going to want to have your own style. This can help to set you apart from other blogs in your niche. It can also keep your readers coming back because they will be used to your style and will want to see what you have to say all the time.

Many bloggers automatically know exactly what they want their content to sound like. Perhaps you have a distinctive personality or set of opinions and you want that to carry through on your blog. Some people prefer to be controversial, whereas other people prefer to just comment in their own voice on the things going on. It is definitely up to you. However, you do need to fine-tune the things you say to what your readers will respond to the most.

One thing you can do is visit other blogs that are already established in your niche. Take notes on the blogger's style and how they differ from other blogs in the niche. Do you like one person's style of writing over the other? What makes a certain blog stand out above others in the niche? Although you definitely don't want to copy anyone's style, doing this exercise can help you generate ideas to become more creative with your writing.

Following are a few common styles you might want to choose from for your blog:

+ **Humorous**—Many people like to find humor in everyday situations. Even if you deal with a difficult niche topic in which people have certain problems, you can inject some humor into things on occasion. People love funny, and you can let your humor fly in your writing.

+ **Controversial**—Certain niches can be controversial. People come back time and time again because they can't get enough. Perhaps they completely agree with you, or perhaps they think you are an idiot. No matter what, it can help to increase your readership and the number of people who link to your blog posts from all around the Web. Be honest; people love a good controversy.

+ **Informative**—Many bloggers find that the people in their niche respond to informative, helpful information. You definitely don't have to be dry when using this style. You can write in a friendly tone that showcases your personality. Talk to people as a friend, and share as much helpful content as possible.

Consider what works best for you before you sit down to write your content. After you do, you will have an overall easier time with writing and coming up with ideas because you will have developed your own style.

 Related Questions

➧ 6. Who is my target audience? **Page 20**

➧ 7. Am I reflecting my brand? **Page 22**

➧ 77. Why does what I do in the real world matter? **Page 216**

➧ 97. How can I build influence? **Page 258**

Action Item

➧ Try writing one post in three different tones. Then write a second post in the tone you liked best. The tone you feel most comfortable with is the one you should work on and develop into something you can call your own.

Importance

26. What Is Google Reader?

Google Reader is one of the most efficient, clean-looking RSS feed readers online. If you already have a Google account, you've already done most of the work involved in setting up your own Google Reader account. If you don't have a Google account already, setting one up is simple. If you don't use Gmail, fear not. You can create a Google account with your current email address. Step-by-step directions for setting up your Gmail account, can be found online. Read Google's tutorial called "How to Set Up a Gmail Account."

Go to Google's Create an Account page. Fill out the form and submit it. In a few seconds, check your email and click on the confirmation link. Presto! You have a Google account. Your sign in name will be your email address.

Google Reader Settings

When you sign into your account page, the first link at the top left will be Google Reader. Click the link next to it that says Settings. From the settings page, you can customize Google Reader to your liking. From the Settings panel, you can click on one of five tabs: Preferences, Subscriptions, Folders and Tags, Goodies, and Import/Export. If you're new to using a feed reader, I suggest sticking with the default options. As you use Google Reader, you'll learn what you like and what you don't, then you can start changing settings to the way you want them.

Preferences

This tab covers the basic options. Select your language. Set Google Reader Home Page to show all items or only certain items, like ones you've starred. Select or deselect the Scroll Tracking option to choose whether the reader marks items as read while you scroll past them or not. Choose whether to always start showing the navigation pane. You can also choose to confirm when marking all your topics as read, and to show followed blogs from Blogger.

Folders and Tags

The Subscriptions tab and Folders and Tags will be empty right now. Once you've added some feeds, you can use these tabs to organize or edit your feeds. Folders and Tags also allows you to choose privacy settings for individual tags. This is setting is really useful when you have lots of feeds for different purposes.

Goodies

From this tab you can add Google Reader to your Google Homepage. It also lets you drag and drop Google Reader to a bookmark. You can use Next Bookmark by clicking a single link. Each time you click the link, you will taken to your next unread item. You can add Google Reader to your cell phone from this tab. There is also a link to drag to your toolbar that will add a bookmark to your toolbar. When viewing a web page, just click the link to view it in Google Reader.

Import/Export

For more advanced users, you can import your feeds from another reader. Just export them in OPML format and save to your computer. Sign into Google Reader, click Settings, Import/Export. Click the Browse button, find your OPML file, and then upload it. You can also export Google Reader feeds from this tab if you are switching to another reader.

Add Feeds

From the Settings panel, click Go to Google Reader. From this page, you can click Take a Tour, or watch a video a Google engineer, Chris Wetherell, tell all about Google Reader. If you're new to feed readers, both those options are worthwhile. For those who are familiar with feed readers, it's really unnecessary to bother with the tour and video. When you're ready, click "Get started by adding subscriptions." Google has some pre-selected bundles of feeds in a few different categories. Newbies should select one of these to play around with Google Reader a little bit. This page also allows new users to quickly add feeds from

Flickr, Blogger, del.icio.us, Live Journal, Windows Live Spaces, Xanga, Wordpress.com, and MySpace by typing in a username, selecting a website from the pull-down menu, and clicking Subscribe.

If you've been following through step-by-step, then your Google Reader account is all set up and ready to use. Whenever you see a little orange RSS link, click it to add to Google Reader.

Note About Privacy

If you have a Gmail account, Google Reader automatically shares all your shared items with all the Google Reader users in your address book. You should manually control this by selecting friends. Click Sharing Settings, on the left sidebar menu. From that page, you can choose whether to share with everyone or just friends. Choose friends by their email address, or remove people from your sharing list completely. If you use Gmail for professional emails or you just want to keep your shared items private from any particular people, I suggest you check out these settings before you start sharing.

 Related Questions

→ 35. What is a blogroll? **Page 105**

→ 36. What are the benefits of sharing other people's articles? **Page 108**

→ 64. What sites can help me find relevant news? **Page 176**

→ 65. What is social bookmarking? **Page 181**

Action Item

→ Go to Google Reader at **www.google.com/reader**, create an account, and subscribe to your first RSS feed.

27. What Do Bloggers Have the Most Trouble With?

Importance

There are several issues that can come up when blogging. When you start a blog, you often have a lot of enthusiasm and ideas for writing. However, as the blog gets older, it can become harder to come up with original ideas for articles and lead to writer's block. Because most bloggers have the goal of writing daily, this burnout can be dangerous because readers have an expectation regarding content and frequency of writing. If the writing becomes more sporadic because of the lack of ideas, visitors will find that it's more difficult to keep track of when updates are made and will often find themselves going to other sites instead.

Another related problem is the thought that all articles must be original. With so many millions of bloggers, original content can be scarce. I mean, really, only so many blogs can write about the newest smart phone before a reader just finds the content really repetitive.

A way to get around this issue is to create an editorial calendar. Brainstorming and documenting ideas for articles and when to use them will help to ensure that you have pre-selected content for certain dates. As news breaks and interesting things happen in the world, content can always be added to the calendar.

 Related Questions

➜ 24. What do I write about? **Page 83**

➜ 25. What tone should I use? **Page 86**

➜ 82. How do I handle inappropriate comments? **Page 228**

➜ 99. How do I keep from being overwhelmed? **Page 263**

Action Item

➜ Create an editorial calendar using whatever calendaring application you prefer. If you don't want to use an actual calendar, create a text document and list out dates. Schedule at least three months worth of posts by indicating the title of the post on each date. Remember that you are aiming for at least one blog post per week at minimum.

Importance

Bulleted lists are also helpful for in-person presentations. Their brevity allows you to highlight the main points on your visual aids while verbally supporting the points in your spoken content.

28. Should I Use Lists?

Lists can often give bloggers a chance to create quick content that interests users and gives immediate satisfaction. Because attention spans are greatly reduced by the influx of technologies like Twitter, lists are easily digestible and can almost have as much impact as a full article.

It is always a good move to use bullet points in a blog post when you can. It is also always a good move to put the key points and takeaways of your post into bullet points so that your readers can pick up on the substance of your post, even if they decide not to read the entire post.

Bullet points can also "lighten" up a post by giving it a feeling of more space, keeping you more concise in your writing, and giving the reader's eyes a break.

Related Questions

➤ 24. What do I write about? **Page 83**

➤ 27. What do bloggers have the most trouble with? **Page 91**

➤ 98. How can I keep my social media efforts interesting? **Page 261**

➤ 99. How do I keep from being overwhelmed? **Page 263**

Action Item

➤ For your first list post, create a list of the top 10 blogs in your subject area—a useful task for yourself while also making readers aware of your existence.

29. How Often Should I Write?

Importance

So you started a blog and you are excited about it, so excited that on the first day of having it, you publish four or five posts. The second day, you throw up another four posts and continue doing that for the next week or so. Now your blog is on its third week, and you are a little burned out, so you decide to skip a few days... hey, you have all that content from before, so you have time, right? The sixth and seventh weeks roll around, and you still haven't added a new post—this is now a problem. Although skipping days or weeks in between posts is not always a bad thing and will not necessarily "hurt" your blog, you can lose some relevancy you gathered in the first couple of weeks. By skipping two or more weeks, you run the risk of the search engines not visiting your site as often as they used to when you were doing a post each day or week.

If you have the time and man power, doing one blog post a day can help your site the most. This isn't always an easy task to accomplish, though, so take it slow and try to do one or two blog posts a week for starters. If you have the time and a go-for-it attitude, aim for four to seven blog posts a week. Just try not to wait more than a week without a fresh post or updated content.

Lack of Inspiration

If you have trouble finding something to write about, you might have picked the wrong niche to be in. You should always have something to talk about; the only exception to this rule is if you created you blog based off a hot topic and then that hot topic completely died. Sadly, if that's the case, you will most likely have to just drop the blog.

Many tools on the web can help you in your search for blog post topics. Keyword tools can enable you to put in a keyword to see what questions people put into the search engines on a particular topic. Consider Google Trends, which tells you what the hot topics are for the day, week, month, or year. Finally, Twitter hot trends can supply you with what people talk about at that given time. These are great tools to utilize when trying to come up with a blog post.

Remember, too, that if you are one of the first blogs to write about a particular topic, you run the risk of getting an absurdly high amount of traffic. If that is something you want (which you should), use these tools.

Posts on Hot Topics

If you have the time to consistently post updates on a hot topic by all means do it. Just remember to blog as much as possible until that topic is dead. Remember though, you don't want to spam either. If you can write only a few sentences on a topic, it isn't worth doing a whole blog post about it. This is where you can also capitalize on your Twitter profile. By posting those one to two sentences about that hot topic, you have a good chance of people who are monitoring that topic to see your tweet, check out your profile, and therefore see your website.

It's been three weeks (or more) since you last updated your blog; is all hope lost? No way. The beauty of blogs is that you might have missed a month or so but with a little elbow grease, you can be back up on the search engines within a couple weeks. You just have to put in the time and put on your "try hard" pants and get a blog post out every day or every other day to make up for the lost time. Soon enough, the search engines will come crawling back to your site and you will see the results again.

 Related Questions

- 27. What do bloggers have the most trouble with? **Page 91**
- 36. What are the benefits of sharing other people's articles? **Page 108**
- 98. How can I keep my social media efforts interesting? **Page 261**
- 99. How do I keep from being overwhelmed? **Page 263**

Action Item

- Practice writing several times a week. Even if you don't publish these pieces on your blog, you'll establish the routine of writing frequently.

30. Are Webinars Valuable?

Importance

Think about a webinar as a way to attend a conference without leaving home. Using your computer and telephone, you can listen to a presentation (such as a conference call) and see the presenter's slides (watching it over an Internet connection). Most of the time you won't be able to see the presenter, the moderator, or others attending the program, and they won't be able to see you.

For most webinars, you need to register ahead of time to reserve your space and obtain instructions for how to join the program on the scheduled day and time.

Just before the scheduled time of the presentation, sign on to the URL specified for the webinar in the confirmation email you receive. You'll have to download some software to your computer. This software gives you the ability to see the presenters' slides on your computer plus any highlighting or drawing they might do during the presentation. In most cases, before the program beings, you'll also dial in to a conference call line using a telephone and password number provided for that particular program. You'll probably hear music (or it will be silent) until the program begins.

Different types of webinar software offer different features, but on most, you can type questions for the presenter and sometimes ask questions or make comments by telephone. You might be asked to respond (during the program) to polling questions; if so, you'll see the responses of other participants, too.

So, what are the benefits to you to host and put on a webinar? There are many, some of which are:

+ Webinars are the easiest to achieve high-value content your brand can generate; it is the easiest way to share expertise and experience, and if you have staff, you can share in a way that can be accessed continuously by prospects visiting your website.

+ People like to hear things from people, not faceless brands. Webinars give you the opportunity for visitors to your website to hear your expertise and experience on specific topics that matter to them, much more so than the generic statements on the website.

+ The invitation to a webinar and the follow-up invitation to download the recorded webinar are valid reasons to email your entire "in-house" list of contacts at least twice.

➡ Announcing you are having a webinar increases your credibility on the subject the webinar will focus on. If you stick to a subject that you know well because of both successful experience and passion, you will likely build credibility.

➡ This high-value content is ideal for pushing out to your social media network; the companies winning at social media are the ones contributing content that speaks to their credibility.

➡ Webinars are easier to sell to the gurus that need to host them; getting them to speak for 30–45 minutes on a subject they are an expert on and passionate about is something they do all the time, and it is a much more "natural act" than asking for a whitepaper.

➡ You can use recorded webinars as "conversion elements" to build your list; gate them behind a form on your website and require a name and email address to access them.

➡ You can effectively increase your brand credibility by co-hosting a webinar with one of your more recognized thought leaders in your space.

➡ Webinars can be nimble; if you recognize a shift in your industry or an event that is of significance, you can quickly reach out to your audience with your insight on the topic.

 Related Questions

➡ 22. What can I install on my website to encourage conversations? **Page 75**

➡ 38. What should I do if I don't want a blog? **Page 110**

➡ 66. What are the best sites for video sharing? **Page 183**

➡ 97. How can I build influence? **Page 258**

Action Item

➡ Find a webinar related to your field and attend it. Be sure to ask a question so that you can see how the host responds. If you feel you can create a similar webinar that people will find worthwhile, try hosting one.

31. What Is FriendFeed?

Importance

FriendFeed is a real-time feed aggregator that consolidates the updates from social media and social networking websites, social bookmarking websites, blogs, and micro-blogging updates, as well as any other type of RSS/ Atom feed. The founders are all former Google Inc. employees who were involved in the launch of such services as Gmail and Google Maps.

The goal of FriendFeed according to their website is to make content on the Web more relevant and useful by using existing social networks as a tool for discovering interesting information. It is possible to use this stream of information to create customized feeds to share, as well as originate new posts and discussions, or comment with friends. Users can be an individual, business, or organization.

 Related Questions

➤ 12. What social networks best fit my goals? **Page 40**

➤ 26. What is Google Reader? **Page 88**

➤ 64. What sites can help me find relevant news? **Page 176**

➤ 72. How can I use social media to help my SEO? **Page 199**

Action Item

➤ Go to **www.friendfeed.com** and set up an account.

Importance

32. What Is a CAPTCHA?

A CAPTCHA is a type of test used to ensure that a response is from a person and not generated by a computer. The process usually involves the user being asked to complete a simple test, which a computer program is able to generate and grade. Because other computers are supposedly unable to solve the CAPTCHA, any user entering a correct solution is presumed to be human.

CAPTCHA is sometimes described as a reverse Turing test, because it is administered by a machine and targeted to a human, in contrast to the standard Turing test that is typically administered by a human and targeted to a machine. A common type of CAPTCHA requires the user to type letters or digits from a distorted image that appears on the screen.

The term "CAPTCHA" was coined in 2000 by Luis von Ahn, Manuel Blum, Nicholas J. Hopper, and John Langford (all of Carnegie Mellon University). It is a contrived acronym based on the word "capture" and standing for "Completely Automated Public Turing test to tell Computers and Humans Apart." Carnegie Mellon University attempted to trademark the term, but the trademark application was abandoned on 21 April 2008.

A CAPTCHA is a means of automatically generating challenges that intend to:

➜ Provide a problem easy enough for all humans to solve.

➜ Prevent standard automated software from filling out a form, unless it is specially designed to circumvent specific CAPTCHA systems.

A check box in a form that reads "check this box please" is the simplest (and perhaps least effective) form of a CAPTCHA. CAPTCHAs do not have to rely on difficult problems in artificial intelligence, although they can. This has the benefit of distinguishing humans from computers. It also creates incentive to further develop the artificial intelligence of computers.

CAPTCHAs are used in attempts to prevent automated software from performing actions which degrade the quality of service of a given system, whether due to abuse or resource expenditure. CAPTCHAs can be deployed to protect systems vulnerable to e-mail spam, such as the webmail services of Gmail, Hotmail, and Yahoo! Mail.

CAPTCHAs are also used to minimize automated posting to blogs, forums, and wikis, whether as a result of commercial promotion, harassment, or vandalism. CAPTCHAs also serve an important function in rate limiting. Automated usage of a service might be desirable until such usage is done to excess and to the detriment of human users. In these cases, administrators can use CAPTCHA to enforce automated usage policies based on given thresholds. The article rating systems used by many news websites are another example of an online facility vulnerable to manipulation by automated software.

As of 2010, most CAPTCHAs display distorted text that is difficult to read by character recognition software. The alternative implementations include various tests, such as identifying an object that does not belong in a particular set of objects, locating the center of a distorted image, or identifying distorted shapes.

What if you can't see well? Because CAPTCHAs rely on visual perception, users unable to view a CAPTCHA (for example, due to a disability) will be unable to perform the task protected by a CAPTCHA.

Therefore, sites implementing CAPTCHAs might provide an audio version of the CAPTCHA in addition to the visual method. The official CAPTCHA site recommends providing an audio CAPTCHA for accessibility reasons, but it is not usable for deaf/blind people or for users of text web browsers. This combination is not universally adopted, with most websites offering only the visual CAPTCHA, with or without providing the option of generating a new image if one is too difficult to read.

Related Questions

➜ 22. What can I install on my website to encourage conversations? **Page 75**

➜ 27. What do bloggers have the most trouble with? **Page 91**

➜ 84. How do I prevent spam? **Page 234**

➜ 85. Can I stop people from hacking? **Page 237**

Action Item

➜ Install a CAPTCHA on your website. There are many out there that can be used. Try **recaptcha.org**, whose service helps "digitize books."

33. How Can Ping.fm Make My Life Easier?

Importance

At the time of this writing, Ping.fm supports 42 social networking sites and services. The premise is simple; you sign up for Ping.fm, add your login credentials for each of the sites you are part of, and start posting. Signing up for and all of the services it supports are free, so there's no reason not to get a few under your belt.

Ping.fm simplifies your life by enabling access to your desired services and allowing you to post once to your Ping account via the website or desktop. Your message instantly becomes available to all of your social sites. They also allow you to post your messages from a slew of other sources like Skype, SMS from your cell phone, GoogleTalk, Yahoo!, or right from your phone.

 Related Questions

➤ 12. What social networks best fit my goals? **Page 40**

➤ 13. How do I choose which sites to use? **Page 52**

➤ 67. How can I share pictures? **Page 187**

➤ 99. How do I keep from being overwhelmed? **Page 263**

Action Item

➤ Go to **www.ping.fm** to set up an account. Make sure that you have all the access points to the various networks you want to connect to. You'll need that in order to fully set up your account.

Importance

34. Should I "Guest Blog?"

Blogging can be an excellent opportunity for an individual to become an expert on a topic. Whether you know a wealth of information about woodworking or your favorite hobby is coin collecting, there is likely a blog on your hobby or favorite activity.

Although most individuals are not going to become famous blogging overnight, individual bloggers can increase their notoriety and buzz by guest blogging on larger blogs in their niche.

Increasing Buzz

Buzz is important on the Internet. Readers want to read blogs that are written by individuals with authority. Although a well written blog is important, individuals couldn't care less if you have nothing credible backing up your blog.

Guest blogging on a major blog in your industry can help to increase buzz around your blog. The more visitors a blogger receives, the higher likelihood that they will ask you to continue guest blogging for them in the future.

Networking

Networking is important in any line of business. However, networking with other bloggers can open up a wide range of opportunities. Bloggers might be able to share stories or even tips on how to improve their content. Blog owners who network are also able to increase readership on their respective blogs. Some guest bloggers are so excellent at writing content that they are compensated for their efforts.

Hopefully the blog that you are guest blogging on is about something you are passionate about. For example, why would you guest blog for a blog on plastic when your passion is collecting sports memorabilia?

Bloggers need to be aware of what they are writing about so that they do not get boring. Ask someone else to read your blog entry before you submit it. Content that engages is important. However, bloggers do not want to have an all-out war about your topic so be sure to keep the topic within reason.

Although one link might bring in new visitors, your name is exposed to all of the readers on this new blog. Readers can research your name and visit your blog. Be sure to write powerful content so that readers are enticed to visit your blog!

Expanding Your Audience

When you post a guest post on another blog, an entirely new audience reads your blog. Your guest blog becomes your new showcase where your expertise, knowledge, and subject authority are made apparent. Ensure that your blog has good content and great design to attract more readers. With the right techniques, you can turn most of your new audience members into regular readers of your blog.

Obtaining Backlinks

Any good content marketer will know that backlinks get your site greater search engine rankings. When you guest blog creatively and intelligently, the blog owner will be happy to provide a backlink to your blog. The blog owner gets more readers to their site owing to your blog and the backlinks ensure that your site gets more traffic. It's a win-win situation for both the guest blogger and the blog owner.

Community Collaboration

Guest bloggers who are able to write powerful content are going to become established members of the community. They will become well-liked and will be invited to a number of opportunities. Networking is important but having a large group of friends can ensure that many doors are opened for a blogger.

Some guest bloggers are able to include a link back to their blog in their guest post. This is an excellent way to receive new visitors to the guest blogger's blog as well as increase the search engine optimization of the guest blogger. Who knows what one link might be able to do!

▶ Different Viewpoints on the Same Topic

Guest posts allow individuals to share different viewpoints on the same topic. For example, one expert might believe individuals need to exercise more than diet. Another expert might believe the exact opposite. Being able to bring these views to the table can provoke discussion within the community and offer excellent information to the readers.

 Related Questions

➡ 24. What do I write about? **Page 83**

➡ 71. How does link building help my website? **Page 197**

➡ 72. How can I use social media to help my SEO? **Page 199**

➡ 97. How can I build influence? **Page 258**

Action Item

➡ Reach out to a blog you admire and ask to be a guest blogger. Be sure to have writing samples or links to your writing samples online so that you can assure the blog publisher of your qualifications.

35. What Is a Blogroll?

Importance

A blogroll is a list of links to blogs that the blogger likes. A blogroll is usually included in the blog's sidebar. Some bloggers split their blogrolls into categories.

A blogroll can be set up by a blogger on any subject or niche and can list any number of bloggers on that blogroll. Updating a blogroll depends on the priority factor given to it. Other factors are also important for you to know as a blogger considering a blogroll.

Blogroll Etiquette of Reciprocation

An unwritten rule is followed when dealing with blogrolls. The rule prevalent in the blogosphere is that any blogger putting your link in his blogroll should be thanked, and in reciprocation, you should feature the blogger's link in your blogroll.

Of course not all links need to be reciprocated. There are times when your link is published in a blogroll on a blog not related to your subject or even on a blog that is ambiguous. So the decision is truly yours to encourage a blogroll and it's at your discretion.

Increasing Traffic

When there are links of yours that are featured in other blogrolls on the blogosphere, the possibilities of these links getting clicked is higher. This possibility increases the chances of driving greater traffic to your blog.

The publicity that you stand to gain through the links is huge, provided there are enough blogs willing to list your blog on their blogrolls. The blogs listing your links also need to have some authority in the blogosphere for the publicity to happen.

A blogroll link also becomes an incoming link, which is considered for the blog ranking. If you have a lot of incoming links from high ranking blogs, then based on the Google juice that gets transferred, you will have greater ranking, too.

Creating a Network

When a blogger is linked on your blogroll, you can contact him via mail to let him know that he has been added to your blogroll. The reason you contact is to ensure that the blogger is aware. Not many people track incoming links.

After the blogger starts to promote you on his blog, the chances of people coming to know of your blogroll and wanting to be promoted by you are high. This cross-promotion creates a network of bloggers and this network can grow stronger with many more joining. This network eventually will be authoritative in the niches publishing blogs.

Adding Value for Your Readers

Readers visit your blog for a reason and they stick on because you provide the information they need. This being the case, every additional piece of information that you provide to the bloggers will be slurped up by the readers.

A blogroll is one such value add, where you let your readers know that there are additional venues where information can be gathered. This increases only your standing among the readers.

Incoming Links for SEO

All the blogs that link you in other blogrolls transfer a certain amount of Google juice. This is an advantage to you, knowing that Google and Technorati consider the incoming links while providing you authority.

The more links you get to your blog, and the more links from high-authority blogs, the greater the gain for you and your blog.

Determining What Blogs to Add

When you have a blogroll, it is unavoidable to receive requests from many bloggers to include their blogs. This becomes a sort of task to decide on the blogs that you can feature in your blogroll and the blogs that you cannot.

What becomes more a challenge is to turn down the offer for a link exchange from a small blogger or a blogger with a totally different niche. You have to be polite while turning down; it is also important to cite the reason why you are turning down. This becomes a tightrope walk because people can get offended and might brand you a snob.

Giving Your Google Juice Away

As advantageous as it is to be linked to by other blogs, the same can be said of blogs that you link to. The blogs that get linked to your blog take away some authority through the outgoing links.

It is important for us to understand and effectively work towards getting incoming links from high-authority blogs and passing them down to low-authority blogs. In this bargain you get to retain some of the Google juice left to build your authority.

 Related Questions

→ 14. Why do I need to be selective? **Page 56**

→ 34. Should I "guest blog?" **Page 102**

→ 68. What is SEO? **Page 190**

→ 71. How does link building help my website? **Page 197**

Action Item

→ Make a list of your five favorite blogs and add these to your blogroll.

Importance

36. What Are the Benefits of Sharing Other People's Articles?

Sharing other people's articles has similar benefits to a blogroll. By providing contextual links back to other sites, you're telling search engines that these particular links are of useful information and relevance to the context you place it in. Those article authors will receive notification of your shared article, and you open up the possibility of being linked to back.

Take a look at what you're sharing on your Twitter or Facebook feeds. If you find that you're often sharing links and making comments on them, you may want to consider making those comments on your own blog, linking to the original article on your blog, and then sharing the link to your own article instead of the original. This can help draw traffic to your own site while taking advantage of the pre-developed content. Because you're sending visitors to the original article, you're also helping to drive traffic to the original author and you may receive rewards from this in the terms of returned traffic.

 Related Questions

➔ 24. What do I write about? **Page 83**

➔ 42. What should I tweet about? **Page 120**

➔ 65. What is social bookmarking? **Page 181**

➔ 71. How does link building help my website? **Page 197**

Action Item

➔ Tweet an interesting post or create your own blog post around an article you like with a link back, and give credit to the original author.

37. Are There Any Tips or Tricks to Interacting on Other Websites?

Importance

Letting bloggers know that you're reading their content can be useful for several reasons. The immediate benefit is that the author you are communicating with can see that you read the story and have taken an interest in what they have to say.

Most importantly, however, your interaction with a blog or website can speak great volumes about your brand. It will allow others to gauge how well you understand different topics and how you can handle direct comments and criticism from people with whom you may not normally interact.

 Related Questions

➡ 82. How do I handle inappropriate comments? **Page 228**

➡ 84. How do I prevent spam? **Page 234**

➡ 86. What do I do if someone is upset by other comments? **Page 240**

➡ 97. How can I build influence? **Page 258**

Action Item

➡ Practice commenting on another site. Be sure it is a comment of value and not just a link back to your own site.

Importance

38. What Should I Do if I Don't Want a Blog?

There are many reasons why you might not want a blog. The most common reason that people don't want to have a blog is that it can be somewhat intimidating to have to develop the blog, figure out what content to include, and then attract and build subscribers.

If you don't want a blog, it's okay! You don't have to have one. But remember that it will be more difficult to drive people to your website if you don't have fresh, updated content.

Without a blog, you'll have to focus on developing other online profiles. Use Twitter and take advantage of hashtags if you want to discuss a particular topic. Utilize Facebook's Notes feature to write longer pieces of content in a way that is similar to a blog but doesn't come with expectations for regular updates. Try social bookmarking services to show other people what you're reading and still establish yourself as an industry leader.

 Related Questions

➔ 22. What can I install on my website to encourage conversations? **Page 75**

➔ 30. Are webinars valuable? **Page 95**

➔ 66. What are the best sites for video sharing? **Page 183**

➔ 71. How does link building help my website? **Page 197**

Action Item

➔ Create a video, podcast, or audio recording and see if this type of content works better for you.

Chapter 6
Twitter

In this chapter:

?

Importance

39. Why Are People Flocking to Twitter?

Twitter (see Figure 6-1) could be considered one of the social networking sites that really kick-started the whole social media revolution. Twitter was founded in 2006 with the purpose of being used by a private team of developers. It was at the 2007 SXSW Conference in Austin, Texas, where it became renowned. Its number of users tripled in just one day and has not slowed down since. So, why is Twitter so popular? The answer to this is as follows:

➤ It's simple.

➤ It's ideal for people who are mobile.

➤ Your friends are on it.

➤ You have access to the mainstream.

➤ Celebrities use it.

FIGURE 6-1: Twitter page

You can choose from many other microblogging services than Twitter, and more show up every day trying to gain popularity. Yet, the thing about Twitter that makes it so successful is it is so simple. Twitter's interface does not offer you much in terms of bells and whistles. You do not have to be super tech savvy because it is easy to understand.

All you need to do is type your message into the box using 140 characters or less and press the Update button. The web interface for viewing
your friends' tweets is simple because it consists of only a reversed
chronologically ordered timeline of tweets.

If you are a little more on the side of being tech-oriented, Twitter has
some advanced features that include things such as searches, trends,
and favorites. More third-party applications can help to expand the
functionality of the platform by adding multicolumn views and an
analysis of tweets. Yet, when you break it down, the core simplicity of
Twitter remains.

Another thing that has helped Twitter grow in popularity is that it
opened up its API to all third-party applications. When this happened,
developers began to create applications that let you do about anything
you can imagine. For instance, if you want to see all of your Twitter
feeds (main feed, replies, direct messages, and other lists) at a glance
on your computer desktop, you can use TweetDeck or Seesmic. If you
want to post a tweet while in the car or on a plane, you can do so via
short message service (SMS), Echofon, Twitter mobile, or Hootsuite.
By enabling developers to create applications for all devices, Twitter
became popular with people who are mobile.

The key moment for any social media service is when it gets so
much buzz and acceptance that all your friends are there. After that
happens, there's no point in using other services because you will have
to either invite them or wait for them to join. The average person does
not go out and join every new social networking site that comes out or is
recommended. Because there are so many people on Twitter, it is likely
you already know a few people who use it. Celebrities, sports stars, poli-
ticians, and cities use it, too. In short, almost anyone who matters to you
is already on Twitter. So there is no incentive to join any other social
networking site that is like it.

Twitter has made appearances in major traditional publications
such as *The New York Times, Time Magazine, People, Entertainment
Weekly, San Francisco Chronicle*, and many others. It is prominent on
NBC News and *CNN*. This acceptance has happened because these
organizations have found that Twitter is a good tool to transmit information. For instance, Twitter was one of the tools citizens of Iran used
to spread the word about alleged election fraud in its last presidential

elections. Twitter isn't replacing mainstream media in being a reliable source of news, but it is becoming a good medium for transmitting information as it happens.

With the increase of gossip magazines, Perez Hilton, and TMZ, it is quite safe to say that people are obsessed with celebrities. So, because of those celebrities who have embraced the site, they are using it to reach out to the public. Fans can now read updates from celebrity Twitter users. It enables fans to feel closer to the star and get information directly from the celebrity. The fans can get great insight, and the celebrities can address rumors, sell product, and just ,well, seem more human.

Many celebrity Twitter accounts are maintained by publicists and media agents, but you can tell that a lot are updated by the owners. Twitter gives celebrities a voice that's surprisingly genuine.

Related Questions

→ 6. Who is my target audience? **Page 20**

→ 12. What social networks best fit my goals? **Page 40**

→ 42. What should I tweet about? **Page 120**

→ 97. How can I build influence? **Page 258**

Action Item

→ Go to Twitter.com and set up an account. Post your first tweet before following anyone.

40. What Is the Difference Between Following and Followers?

Importance

Following people on Twitter means that you subscribe to their account; this is called being a follower. Therefore, when the people you follow post something on their account, it appears in your timeline (see Figure 6-2). When you follow a person, you are allowing that person to send you a private message called a *direct message*. Only you and the sender can see the direct message.

FIGURE 6-2: A typical view of a following page on Twitter

As an example, pretend you follow @barrymoltz. You can see his updates in your timeline and receive any direct messages that Barry may send you. Now, unless Barry follows you, you cannot send Barry a direct message nor can he see your updates in his timeline.

Followers are people who request to have your tweets show up in their timeline and allow you to send them direct messages. If you follow someone, you are their follower. Thus, if you follow @barrymoltz, you are his follower.

> When a person follows you and you reciprocate, you are friends. So, if you follow me, and I follow you, we are each other's friends on Twitter.

Related Questions

Action Items

➜   Look at your Followers Page and your Following Page to see
    how they are different.

➜   Locate the pages for Lists, Mentions, and DMs.

41. How Do I Increase My Twitter Following?

Importance

Twitter is more than personal updates. Sure, you can find people who pass random information such as what their cats are doing, that they are listening to a Michael Jackson song, or they just ate the most amazing cheeseburger. Yet, at a deeper level you can use Twitter for much more than that. Twitter has created opportunities for people to communicate in a different way; using Twitter, people (as both individuals and brand representatives) can microblog to establish connections, nurture relationships, and build reputations. Because of the character limit, the way people communicate has become more efficient. Microblogging has reduced the time to syndicate content down to mere seconds. People continue to utilize Twitter for this purpose because as content continually gets refined for this compacted communication tool, they've found that Twitter can be a great tool to

- Share breaking news.
- Find employees.
- Get answers to questions.
- Get product feedback.
- Vent.
- Promote yourself.
- Promote others.

> A *microblog* is one that enables up to 140-character-long posts. Twitter is the most popular and enables text messaging for blog postings via cell phones.

Rule of Thumb   The best way to increase your followers is to start tweeting. Look at what people talk about, jump in with some @s (replies to a user) and some direct messages, too.

▶ RSS Versus Twitter

When you post a link to your latest blog post to Twitter, you are doing a *push*. You are trying to grab the readers. Readers may ignore it, but those followers who like what you post can check out your article within seconds. RSS on the other hand is a *pull*. Users check their RSS feeds out when they want to check them. It can take days or weeks for people to read what you write.

People increase their follower base in many different ways. Some of the best and most simple ways follow:

→ When you post a link, sometimes put "Please RT" at the end of the post. RT or retweet is the act of taking what someone posted and reposting it in your timeline. Retweeting pushes your @ username into different timelines, which can cause people to check your profile.

→ Use a complete Twitter bio. Your latest tweets and @replies don't mean much to someone who doesn't know you. Your bio is the only place you have to tell people who you are. Leaving it blank or cryptic doesn't encourage people to add you.

→ Put links to your Twitter profile whenever you join a new website or social network. This includes LinkedIn, Facebook, your blog, in your email signature, YouTube, and almost anywhere.

→ Tweet about your interests, hobbies, and things that get you fired up in life; then *hashtag* them.

→ Mention your Twitter account whenever you can. Every time you give a talk, speak on a panel, produce a podcast, write a guest blog post, create slides, or hand out business cards, figure out a way to broadcast or display your twitter account.

→ Share pictures. Pictures are heavily retweeted.

→ Follow the top twitter users and watch what they tweet. Pay attention to the types of content they send out and how they interact with their followers.

People use the hashtag symbol **#** before relevant keywords in their tweet to categorize those tweets to show more easily in Twitter Search. Hashtags can be applied to any conversation you want to be able to easily review or follow later, regardless if the subject matter is offline or online.

Related Questions

→ 40. What is the difference between "followers" and "following?" **Page 115**

→ 57. Should I link my Facebook and Twitter accounts? **Page 159**

→ 90. What are key influencers? **Page 247**

→ 97. How can I build influence? **Page 258**

Action Items

➤ Respond to at least three tweets written by other people.

➤ Share one article.

➤ Follow back at least five people who already follow you.

Importance

42. What Should I Tweet About?

Determining what to tweet about is probably one of the most difficult parts about being on Twitter. Many people are skeptical about the service because with so many millions of users, a voice can easily get lost in the crowd.

When starting out, sometimes the best thing to do is just listen. Open up your account and figure out whom you want to follow. Check out leaders in your industry, potential competitors, and potential consumers, and then follow people with the same personal interests as you. Then, just start reading what they write. You may find that you want to respond to their comments or pass what they write off to other people to enjoy. As you start to do so, you'll find that what you're actually doing is engaging with the people you're following. As you become more comfortable, you'll gradually start to figure out what kind of content works best for you.

In general, the different types of content you can share are:

➜ News (current events)

➜ Articles about your industry

➜ Retweets of other content you like

➜ Responses to other people

➜ Comments about interesting things you hear or see that are relevant to your audience

When possible, it's always good to have much of your content include responses to others or personal commentary. It shows that your brand is human and responsive.

Klout, the online influence measurement service, defines user influence styles in 16 different categories that help to let others understand what type of content may come through the account (see Figure 6-3). Following is an excerpt from the Klout.com website to help you understand what each of the different styles are:

➜ Celebrity (for example, @barackobama or @aplusk)

    You can't get any more influential than this. People hang on your every word and share your content like no other. You're probably famous in real life and your fans simply can't get enough.

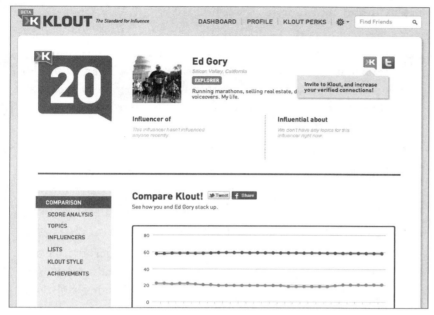

FIGURE 6-3: A Klout profile

→ Taste Maker (for example, @missrogue)

You know what you like and your audience likes it too. You know what's trending, but you do more than just follow the crowd. You have your own opinion that earns respect from your followers.

→ Pundit (for example, @scobleizer)

You don't just share news, you create the news. As a pundit, your opinions are wide-spread and highly trusted. You're regularly recognized as a leader in your industry. When you speak, people listen.

→ Thought Leader (for example, @chrissaad)

You are a thought leader in your industry. Your followers rely on you, not only to share the relevant news, but to give your opinion on the issues. People look to you to help them understand the day's developments. You understand what's important and what your audience values.

→ Broadcaster (for example, @huffingtonpost)

You broadcast great content that spreads like wildfire. You are an essential information source in your industry. You have a large and diverse audience that values your content.

➤ Curator (for example, @chrisbrogan)

You highlight the most interesting people and find the best content on the web and share it to a wide audience. You are a critical information source to your network. You have an amazing ability to filter massive amounts of content to surface the nuggets that your audience truly cares about. Your hard work is very much appreciated.

➤ Feeder (for example, @loldrivers)

Your audience relies on you for a steady flow of information about your industry or topic. Your audience is hooked on your updates and secretly can't live without them.

➤ Syndicator (for example, @DrShock)

You keep tabs on what's trending and who's important to watch. You share the best of this with your followers and save them from having to find what's hot on their own. You probably focus on a specific topic or cater to a defined audience.

➤ Networker (for example, @lewishowes)

You know how to connect to the right people and share what's important to your audience. You generously share your network to help your followers. You have a high level of engagement and an influential audience.

➤ Socializer (for example, @bobbrisco)

You are the hub of social scenes and people count on you to find out what's happening. You are quick to connect people and readily share your social savvy. Your followers appreciate your network and generosity.

➤ Specialist (for example, @joefernandez)

You might not be a celebrity, but in your area of expertise your opinion is second to none. Your content is likely focused around a specific topic or industry with a focused, highly-engaged audience.

➤ Activist (for example, @alexlines)

You've got an idea or cause you want to share with the world and you've found the perfect medium for it. Your audience counts on you to champion your cause.

→ Conversationalist (for example, @kuratowa)

You love to connect and always have the inside scoop. Good conversation is not just a skill; it's an art. You might not know it, but when you are witty, your followers hang on every word.

→ Dabbler (for example, @ask500people)

You might just be starting out with the social web or maybe you're not that into it. If you want to grow your influence, try engaging with your audience and sharing more content.

→ Explorer (for example, @nitinchitkara)

You actively engage in the social web, constantly trying out new ways to interact and network. You're exploring the ecosystem and making it work for you. Your level of activity and engagement shows that you "get it." One can predict that you'll be moving up.

→ Observer (for example, @adrockus)

You don't share much, but you follow the social web more than you let on. You may just enjoy observing more than sharing or you're checking this stuff out before jumping in full-force.

 Related Questions

→ 41. How do I increase my Twitter following? **Page 117**

→ 64. What sites can help me find relevant news? **Page 176**

→ 72. How can I use social media to help my SEO? **Page 199**

→ 97. How can I build influence? **Page 258**

Action Item

→ Post a tweet about anything that you feel adequately reflects your brand personality and that you think will get retweeted at least twice.

Importance

43. Why Is Twitter Search So Powerful?

Twitter has a live search feature that can act as a tremendous tool for businesses if utilized to its potential. Usable through the web interface by visiting `http://search.twitter.com` (see Figure 6-4) or through different third-party Twitter tools designed as a search form field, users can perform searches of any keywords, names, or terms of interest. The results are pulled in from the live Twitter stream. Results can even continue to come in as more tweets pass through the filter of your search.

FIGURE 6-4: Twitter real-time search

This is so dramatically different from normal search, such as with Google, Yahoo, or Bing. They are different because searches are performed in real time. The tweets that result from your search are what people are saying right now and through your search, you have the ability to act on it. On the normal search engines, results come from news or information that has already been archived for several days, months, or even years.

Content-wise, this gives you access to the greater Twitter world in terms of finding new and interesting content to share with your audience. You'll likely discover new people through search through your common interests, and proceed to follow them and learn even more.

As a business or brand, what makes Twitter search so powerful is its ability to give you access to people's current questions, concerns, or comments. Your brand now has the opportunity to address those issues in a way that could prove to be beneficial to your brand in terms of new customers or new positioning as a thought leader.

 Related Questions

➡ 6. Who is my target audience? **Page 20**

➡ 43. Why is Twitter search so powerful? **Page 124**

➡ 72. How can I use social media to help my SEO? **Page 199**

➡ 73. How do I track what is said about my brand? **Page 202**

Action Item

➡ Identify three keywords that revolve around your brand or industry. Go to **search.twitter.com** and enter those terms to identify people with similar interests.

Importance

44. What Are Twitter Trends?

Twitter trends (see Figure 6-5) are the topics that most people on the service are talking about *right now*. Like with search, Twitter trends are updated in real time and are filtered for users to list topics of common interest that are hot and exciting to discuss. These topics typically consist of "breaking news" that can be related to current political events, celebrities, new technology, or just general terms or hashtags that people promote and use.

FIGURE 6-5: Twitter trends

A *trending topic* is a word, phrase, or topic that is posted (tweeted) multiple times on Twitter. Trending topics become popular either through a concerted effort by users or because of an event that prompts people to talk about one specific topic.

Trends can be localized to regions, countries, or they can be worldwide. This will let you see what the latest hot news is for a certain locale, which may be more relevant for your brand. According to Twitter.com, cities and countries listed change "dynamically based on tweet volume" and if the country or city is missing, Twitter isn't "receiving enough Tweets from that geographical area to create a quality list."

Related Questions

➤ 39. Why are people flocking to Twitter? **Page 112**

➤ 42. What should I tweet about? **Page 120**

➤ 72. How can I use social media to help my SEO? **Page 199**

➤ 74. What brand monitoring tools can I use? **Page 204**

Action Item

→ Locate the trends column in your Twitter sidebar (on the
right) and post a tweet using one of the trending hashtags.
Do one for global trends and one for your local region
trends.

Chapter 7

Facebook

In this chapter:

45. Why Do So Many People Use Facebook?

Facebook is a social networking website intended to connect friends, families, business associates, and anyone else. It began as a college networking website and has expanded to include the general public (see Figure 7-1).

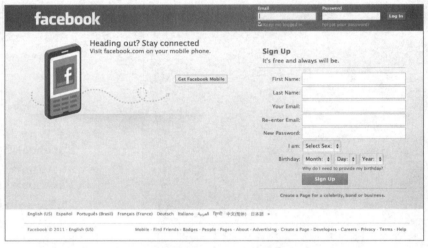

FIGURE 7-1: The Facebook home page

It was founded in 2004 by Harvard student Mark Zuckerberg and originally was called thefacebook. It was quickly successful on campus and expanded beyond Harvard into other Ivy League schools. With the phenomenon growing in popularity, Zuckerberg enlisted two other students, Duston Moskovitz and Chris Hughes, to assist. Within just a few months, Zuckerberg's simple networking project became a nationwide college networking website.

As the site continued growing and the site went national, both Zuckerberg and Moskovitz left Harvard to work full time on the Facebook. In August 2005, after securing the rights to the domain Facebook.com for a reported $200,000, they renamed it Facebook. During this time, access to the site was available only to schools, universities, organizations, and a limited number of companies in English-speaking countries. Since this time, the site has expanded to open registration for anyone who wants to sign up.

Facebook users create a profile page that shows information about themselves to their friends. The profile typically includes the following: Information, Status, Friends, Photos, Likes, and the Wall.

Users can search for friends and acquaintances by email address, school, or by typing in a name or location into search. When people become friends, they can see each other's profiles, including contact information. Email notifications enable users to know when new friends leave a comment, post to their Wall, or send a message to them within the system.

A popular feature on Facebook is the ability to share photographs uploaded from a phone, camera, or computer. As with other private information, users have the option to allow only friends to see their pictures or anyone on the site. An unlimited amount of storage is available, which is a major advantage of Facebook's photograph-sharing capabilities.

Facebook pages can be created by users. These can include anything from companies, products, originations, hobbies, television shows, movies, musicians, and celebrities. Facebook pages can be public and available to everyone or private, so that only those invited can join and view discussions. Similarly, the Events feature in Facebook enables friends to organize parties, concerts, and other get-togethers in the real world.

Countless applications are available to add to a profile, from a list of Top Friends, movie compatibility, games, things you support, maps of where you have traveled—the choice of apps are almost endless. Most of these applications are created by individuals, and are unaffiliated with Facebook.

Users of Facebook can share news stories, video, and other files with friends. Most news and video websites have buttons that can be clicked to automatically share the story or video on a person's profile in Facebook. The persons sharing also have the option to make comments about the shared item that their friends can see.

When sharing an item, users can attach the item to their Wall for all to see or tag an individual person that they think would be most interested in seeing the item. When people are tagged, they receive notification in Facebook or through email letting them know they have been tagged.

Related Questions

Action Item

➡ Set up your personal Facebook profile if you don't already have one. Make sure it's 100 percent complete and check your privacy settings to be sure they are as strict or relaxed as you need them to be.

46. What Are the Different Types of Facebook Pages?

Importance

There are certain technical nuances for setting up a business presence on Facebook that you need to be aware of before you start. Before you spend countless hours frustrated, review the difference between an individual Profile page on Facebook (see Figure 7-2) versus a Facebook page for businesses or brands (see Figure 7-3).

FIGURE 7-2: A Facebook Profile

FIGURE 7-3: A Page on Facebook

Facebook has made a clear distinction between Profiles and Pages. The bottom line: Profiles are only for individuals and Pages are for brands (for example, businesses, entertainment, products, and public figures). Profiles and Pages have different features. Certain features are not permitted for business pages but are available to individual profiles. Businesses are allowed to have only a Page but not a Profile page. A business that opens a Profile is in direct violation of Facebook's Terms of Service (TOS). Some of the differences follow:

➤ Pages enable any Facebook users to "like" the brand, but access to the individual Profile pages is limited.

➤ Pages cannot access the Profiles of its fans. A user can "like" the page without risking privacy issues. If a Profile approves a friend request, that friend's profile is now available for viewing.

➤ A Profile can have only 5,000 friends. Pages can have unlimited "likes."

 Related Questions

➤ 4. How do I develop my brand strategy? **Page 13**

➤ 6. Who is my target audience? **Page 20**

➤ 50. How do I use Facebook analytics? **Page 146**

➤ 56. How do I reach out to other brands on Facebook? **Page 158**

Action Item

➤ Identify a personal Profile and a brand Page and become acquainted with the different formats and features.

47. How Do I Best Use My Facebook Page?

Importance

Facebook is the biggest social networking site and is growing by thousands if not tens of thousands every day. Because of its huge user base, you cannot deny the ease with which a brand can reach its customers and create potential customers. Today, brands are jumping on the Page bandwagon to utilize Facebook because it allows them to boost their brand's reach, influence, and engagement with people. It is convenient for a brand to create a Page and publish its profile and products; however, setting up a Facebook Page that receives many likes and a huge fan base is never an easy task. This section covers some easy things you can do to help increase the number of likes and engagement with the brand.

Make Them Like It First

Most users probably click the Wall or Info, and if nothing is more fascinating than that, chances are they will leave your Page. It is an advantage to you when visitors "like" your page (see Figure 7-4) and then become a true fan. This is because they can then be updated from time to time with the latest things you publish on their timeline. To encourage them to "like" the Page, you can make all non-fans see a landing page first when they arrive at your Page. The main purpose of your Facebook landing page is to convert visitors into fans. You should place a clear call-to-action graphic in the Landing tab to help get more "likes" from your visitors.

Create a Unique Page Image

The profile image of a Page is something a lot of brands do not give a lot of thought to. It is a simple picture that is placed in the border of a 200-pixel-wide box. You might be surprised with the amazing and creative ideas that people come up with.

FIGURE 7-4: The Coca Cola tab makes you like it to unlock the secret.

Tens of thousands of Pages just show the brand's typical standard logo. If you have the resources and time, you should create an engaging and creative image for your Page (see Figure 7-5). It's one of the first things users will see and it has the potential to leave a lasting impression.

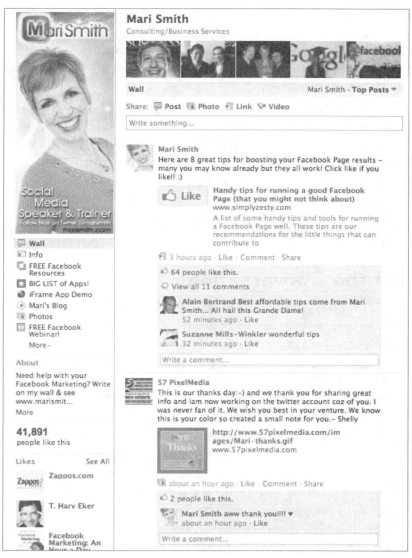

FIGURE 7-5: Mari Smith utilizes her sidebar image to give visitors her Twitter information.

Integrate Applications to Increase Engagement

One of the worst things that can happen is after you spend time and energy to set up a Facebook Page, a person discovers it and then quickly leaves without becoming a fan. The greatest resource you have to capture users' attention is through engaging applications. There are currently more than 75,000 applications on the Facebook platform. A great number of them can be easily added to your Page and are perfect for the small- to medium-sized brand.

If you are a medium-to-large brand, it is a good practice to create a more exciting experience for the fan. By installing applications that have games, quizzes, and other types of dynamic content, you can keep users on your Page for longer durations of time. You live in a short-attention-span world with many distractions, so you want to get all the attention you can from a person. You should ensure that your application has a call to action so that when new users land on the Page, they are immediately engaged (refer to Figure 7-5).

Join the Conversation

Social networking sites such as Facebook have given brands the capability to be part of discussions people have, allowing them to be almost human. That means every time someone comments on your status update, a photo, a video, a discussion thread, or anything else, you need to respond. Long gone are the days of a one-way conversation in which a brand would shout out to its customers. You live in the midst of a conversational revolution and your brand needs to join in.

Failing to engage your customers and even your potential customers now means you're missing out on opportunities. Even worse, it means you may lose out to your competition, which may be engaging with them on a regular basis. Whether you are a small business (dentist, physician, plumber, restaurant, and so on) or a large corporation, you need to be talking and interacting, and the only way to do that is through a regular dialogue. People ask you questions and make comments about what you do. You need to reply and in turn ask them things about how you can improve what you do, how they rate their experience with you, or what they think of your engagement. Then, you can reply to and ask them questions as well. Remember, these are regular folks who do not live and die by your brand, so it's okay—and you're encouraged to talk about things not brand-related.

If you give the extra effort to engage with your fans, you can find that they will give back, engage more, and spread the word about you.

Publish Interesting and Relevant Content

In all areas of social media, you need to provide interesting content to your readers. Facebook is no different than any other tool. By regularly sharing relevant content, your fans will keep returning to your page. While attracting repeat visitors is not the single-most important component of a Page, having repeat engagement is easily one of the most important. In online communities, one of the most effective measurements of the state of a community is that of repeat usage. Facebook Pages and other digital content channels are no different. Fans who return to your Page regularly are significantly more likely to continue engaging with your brand by sharing content and taking action when you call upon them. The bottom line is that a plain, old, boring Facebook Page is not doing you much good.

While it's important to watch the conversations that people have on your Page, you also need to start conversations. By asking questions on your Page, creating new topics on the discussion forums, and sharing interesting articles that create dialogue, you'll keep fans coming back. This is similar to the concept of publishing blog posts regularly on a website to drive traffic. Unless you keep engaging your fans on a regular basis and post interesting content, you are going to find it difficult to continuously attract new fans. "Regular" engagement is going to be different for every Page. You'll have to study your Facebook analytics to get an idea of how often people visit your page, what time they visit and what days are the heaviest in traffic. If you see daily spikes in traffic, you may want to update daily. If you only get a lot of traffic on Sundays, then you'll need to update much less often.

Events provide an amazing opportunity for brands to reach out to their fan base. These events don't actually need to be in-person events! When multiple people RSVP to an event, there are increased odds that your event will be distributed through a social graph, which drives new users to your brand's Page. An event can be an actual occasion, or can be a cause or effort to support (see Figure 7-6).

A *social graph* is a diagram that illustrates interconnections among people, groups, and organizations in a social network. The term refers to both the social network itself and a diagram representing the network.

FIGURE 7-6: An event to attend the online search for a missing person helped to keep this cause at the top of newsfeeds.

 Related Questions

➜ 5. What is my brand's objective? **Page 18**

➜ 25. What tone should I use? **Page 86**

➜ 48. What should my Facebook page be about? **Page 141**

➜ 64. What sites can help me find relevant news? **Page 176**

Action Items

➜ Post a video.

➜ Write a Note.

➜ Upload a photo.

48. What Should My Facebook Page Be About?

Importance

One of the most commonly asked questions about Pages is, "How often should I post to Facebook?" The answer is not clear because it depends on your fans and the subject.

If you have a Page for your business or organization, you should update it two to three times a week when you first launch. It is a good idea to consider posting items of interest to your readers such as useful tips, your latest video or blog post, or even a link to an online news article related to your industry—with your personal take on it.

As you gather more fans and get more of them to interact with your Page postings (or if you're lucky enough to be a celebrity), your Facebook paparazzi are probably hungry to often hear from you about what's happening with your business, events, travel tours, tips, books you've written, and so on. At this point, you can probably increase your posts to two to three postings per day.

You can figure out how well your frequency of posting works by simply monitoring your engagements (fans liking your page postings or commenting on them) and by viewing your Page Insights. If you begin to post more frequently and start noticing a significant increase in the number of people who unsubscribe from your Page, this may be a sign to tone down the number of postings.

Remember that out of sight truly is out of mind, and in this busy world, your brand might often be the last things on people's minds. By posting on a regular basis to your Facebook Page and measuring your results, you'll not only keep your readers up to date with what's happening but you'll also help them crave more tidbits about you and keep you in mind the next time they or someone else they know may need your service or offering.

Related Questions

➜ 5. What is my brand's objective? **Page 18**

➜ 10. How do I brand my online identity? **Page 34**

➜ 12. What social networks best fit my goals? **Page 40**

➜ 88. What does a social media strategy look like? **Page 244**

Action Item

➔ Create your Facebook Page and follow Facebook's step-by-step guide to complete your information.

49. How Do I Get People to Like My Facebook Page?

Importance

Mari Smith from the Social Media Examiner is probably one the smartest Facebook "ninjas" out there. She has compiled hundreds of tips and tricks on the subject of getting people to like a Facebook Page. The first thing she points out is that many people think that after they create a page they should invite all their personal Facebook friends to the page, using the "Suggest to Friends" feature. She points out this is actually not an effective thing to do because of the following:

➜ Many people complain that after they decline a request from a friend, they get asked again and again, finding it irritating.

➜ Facebook users can like only up to 500 pages and might want to be selective.

➜ Page suggestions often build up, unnoticed.

➜ To aggressively pursue all your friends to join your page, for no apparent incentive, is counterintuitive to the nature of social media.

Some of her most creative tips, examples, and great insights include:

➜ **Embed widgets on your website**—Select from a number of the new Facebook social plugins and place them on your website and blog. The Like Box widget works well to display your current Page stream and a selection of fans. Mari Smith recommends adding a title above the box encouraging visitors to your site/blog to click the "Like" button (which makes them a Facebook fan).

➜ **Invite your email and ezine subscribers**—Assuming you have an opt-in email list, send out an invitation to your subscribers via email (several times, over time) letting them know about your page and encouraging them to join. Ideally, provide them with a description of the page and an incentive.

Be sure to have the Facebook logo/badge appear in your HTML newsletters. Instead of the usual "Join our Page," say something creative such as "Write on our Facebook Wall," "Join our Facebook community," or "Come add your photo to our Facebook group" (where "group" is actually your page). Users must be a fan to interact with your page in this way.

- **Add to your email signature block**—Instead of promoting your Facebook personal profile, include a link to your page in every email you send out. If you use web-based email, check out the Wisestamp signature add-on.

- **Make a compelling welcome video**—Create an attractive landing tab (canvas page) with a video that explains exactly what your page is about, who it's for, and why they should become fans. The result: You'll increase your conversion rate from visitors to fans.

- **Integrate the new Facebook comment feature**—Mari Smith's favorite example of a brand's use of the comment feature is from the T-shirt company Threadless. On its landing tab (canvas page), you can view and purchase T-shirts and Like and comment on any item and choose to have that comment posted to your Facebook profile.

  Threadless actually has its landing tab set up so that visitors don't have to become a fan to purchase/comment/interact. Yet, it organically built more than 100,000 fans.

  As users comment on items, that activity is pushed out into fan newsfeeds, which creates valuable viral visibility for your Page.

- **Get fans to tag photos**—If you host live events, be sure to take plenty of photos (or even hire a professional photographer), load the photos to your page, and encourage fans to tag themselves. This, again, pushes out into their Wall and friends' News Feeds, providing valuable (free!) exposure. And a picture says a thousand words—we notice the thumbnails in our feed more than text.

- **Load videos and embed on your site**—Facebook's Video feature is extremely powerful. You can load video content to your Facebook Page, take the source code, and embed on your blog/website. Embedded Facebook videos display a white watermark hotlink of the Facebook name in the upper-left corner of the video. This is a clickable link that goes to the original video page on your Page. If the visitor to your site clicks through to Facebook from your video, and they are logged into Facebook at the time, they see a Like button at the top-left corner of the video player.

➔ **Get fans to join via SMS**—People can join your Page via text message. You need to get your first 25 fans and secure your username. Then, to join your Page, Facebook users simply send a text message to 32665 (FBOOK) with the words (without the quotes) "fan yourusername" or "like yourusername".

This feature is ideal when you address a live audience or large group. You can ask them to pull out their mobile phones and immediately join your Page.

➔ **Use print media**—Look at every piece of print media you use in your business. Your Facebook Page should be clearly displayed. Put your Facebook Page link and logo on your business cards, letterhead, brochures, print newsletters, magazine ads, products, and more.

➔ **Use the Share button**—The Share button is all over Facebook and is a handy feature. It only works for sharing on your personal Profile. So periodically go to your page, scroll toward the bottom-left column, and click the "Share+" button. Add a compelling comment with exciting news, recent changes, special incentives, and so on happening on your page and invite your friends to join if they haven't already. The Share+ button can be far more effective than the Suggest to Friends approach because it provides context.

 Related Questions

➔ 20. Would collecting email addresses be worthwhile? **Page 71**

➔ 23. How do I add a blog to my website? **Page 82**

➔ 76. Do I still need a business card? **Page 214**

➔ 97. How can I build influence? **Page 258**

Action Item

➔ Post a link to your Facebook page on your personal profile, create a link on your website to it, and tweet it!

Importance

50. How Do I Use Facebook Analytics?

Facebook provides all Page administrators with a tool for tracking the growth of the Page. This tool includes the capability to measure interactions on your Page. You can use a few statistics and measurements on the Insights page to help you determine how to improve the traffic on your page.

Facebook provides one metric it suggests Page administrators use to determine the quality of their posts called Post Quality. Facebook recommends that a Page have approximately two to three posts a day. It also states that you can measure the quality of the post by looking at the number of comments and likes you receive per post.

The simplest way to get more engagement on your Page is to ask questions. Facebook insights will use comments, likes, and link clicks among other things to determine the number of these interactions as a percentage of the size of your fan base. If 50 percent or more of your fan base engages with you on a regular base, you then get a high post-quality score.

> The use of humor can go a long way to get comments and likes. It incites people's emotions in a positive way, which helps people to feel positive about your page.

Rule of Thumb   The best model for improving your post quality is to test out various types of posts to see which attract the most responses. Whenever you find a post that attracts a large response, you may want to make it a habit to post similar updates.

Total Fans and Unsubscribed Fans

> Remember, it is quality over quantity!

A helpful Insight graph to watch is the number of fans you have and the number of those that have unsubscribed. Keep a keen eye on those that have unsubscribed. If this number is increasing over time, you may want to review the types of posts you make and the number of posts you make. Although posting regularly is important, you can chase fans away by posting too often.

Interactions

You will find that as the number of fans on your Facebook Page increases, the number of users interacting with your Page will increase as well. These interactions can be comments, Wall posts, or likes. You can track the number of interactions on your Facebook page by viewing the Interactions graph. This graph is one of the more useful ones because it shows you if you are doing a good job engaging with your fans on your Page.

> The Interactions graph is the default graph on your Insights page (see Figure 7-7).

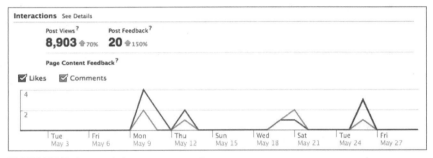

FIGURE 7-7: A sample Interaction graph

> The Interactions per Post chart can help you measure the level of engagement you receive per post. As the number of fans grows on your page, in theory the quality of your posts should improve because you give your fans content they want.

Page Views

The Page View has become one of the standard measures of success on the Internet for websites. It simply shows the number of people that have looked at your Page for any given amount of time. Within Facebook Insights, a Page View shows regardless if a user is a new fan or an existing fan. As your page grows, the total number of daily page views will increase.

Demographics

The Demographics Chart within Insights has the capability to track the demographics of your fan base. Although Facebook has the breakdown of your fans' demographics as percentages, you can also view the absolute number of users within your Facebook Page by their gender, age, and country from which they view your Page. By analyzing the Demographics Chart, you can track which demographic groups are growing quickest and which demographic groups are the largest.

Analytical studies of the Demographics Chart can also serve to reinforce your data surrounding your target market. If it contradicts your target market data, however, it can also serve as support for changing your marketing plan.

 Related Questions

Action Item

→ Go to your Facebook Insights and become acquainted with different buttons and graphs. Export the data and save it for a later resource.

51. What Is Facebook Connect?

Importance

Facebook Connect is a tool that enables a website to access a user's Facebook account. The most common use for Facebook Connect is as a registration system for websites. Because hundreds of millions of people already use Facebook, it makes registering on a new website simple. Facebook Connect enables you to use your Facebook ID and password to sign into websites. After you log in, it pulls your name and photo into the site, completing the registration process for you. It can also look at your Facebook friends to let you connect with any that have signed up for the website you just joined.

A powerful part of this feature is the capability to easily have content you like placed back on your Facebook newsfeed. This content shows up on Facebook as if it were any other Wall posting. The full extent of your activity is listed, along with a link for people to follow.

 Rule of Thumb   If you don't want your data shared with a particular site, don't sign up with it. Or, if you want to use your Facebook account there but not have the information relayed back to your Profile, just check the appropriate box when you initially sign on.

Related Questions

→ 23. How do I add a blog to my website? **Page 82**

→ 52. How do Facebook "likes" help me? **Page 150**

→ 56. How do I reach out to other brands on Facebook? **Page 158**

→ 75. How can social media websites make this easier? **Page 212**

Action Item

→ Install Facebook Connect on your blog or website.

Importance

52. How Do Facebook "Likes" Help Me?

Facebook likes are the simplest way for a user to interact with others on Facebook. Rather than having to comment on a post, users can just click the Like button and indicate that they find the post useful in some way. It's a form of commitment that allows users to still somewhat keep a distance while indicating their approval of a comment or update.

On Facebook, the more that your page is interacted with, the more your posts will be seen on user newsfeeds. As the number of people engaging with you grows, so does your exposure to new potential fans. The greater or more influential the user that interacts with your brand already is, the greater the impact on your Facebook engagement statistics and more likely your post will show up more frequently on the newsfeeds. This act of spreading information from fan to potential fan is the viral aspect of Facebook that brands are so drawn to (see Figure 7-8). It's this potential of tapping into the external connections that your established foundation network already has that excites brands and moves them to develop a strong Facebook presence.

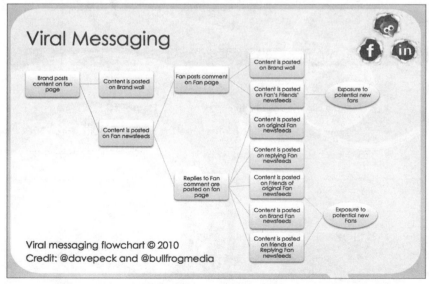

FIGURE 7-8: Facebook activity spreads from friend to friend, creating a tree of activity.

Related Questions

➤ 4. How do I develop my brand strategy? **Page 13**

➤ 23. How do I add a blog to my website? **Page 82**

➤ 37. Are there any tips or tricks to interacting on other websites? **Page 109**

➤ 76. Do I still need a business card? **Page 214**

Action Item

➤ Like a post written by one of your friends and see if it shows up on your home feed.

Importance

53. How Do I Create Events in Facebook?

The world's current largest social network hosts millions of event listings each month and is only getting bigger. These events exist online, offline, are big and small, from corporations to small businesses to birthday parties. In short, they can be any type of event you can imagine.

Creating an Event Listing

You can find the Events feature in several places in Facebook. The easiest ways to access it are the navigational link at the top-left side of your home page or by going to the search feature at the top of any page and just typing Events.

On the Events page, you can view upcoming events that you have been invited to or have created. You can also see events that your friends are attending, past events, and a list of your friends' birthdays.

To create an event, click the Create an Event button. You are then prompted to put in your event's name, location name, start and end times, the location address, and add a picture and detailed description of the event.

> You can also cancel an event, which is an action that can't be undone after it is selected. Facebook does enable you to optionally attach a note to all invitees with reasons why the event was canceled.

Privacy Options

When creating an event, Facebook gives you two options for the event's privacy:

- **Open**—Open events can be seen by anyone, and anyone can RSVP or invite others to the event, regardless of whether they were originally invited.

- **Private**—These events are seen only by those invited, so they won't show up in the news feeds of those who attend, and only invitees can RSVP.

> Facebook Events also have a feature called Show the Guest List. You can toggle whether to allow guests to see who else is invited. When possible, refrain from hiding the guest list. It can help to show it because if users see that their friends are attending, they'll be more likely to attend as well.

Managing and Promoting Your Event

After your event is up and running, you have two options: Let it stagnate and hope people show up, or get actively involved in promotion and management. For anything but a small, private get-together with friends, the latter is usually a better option.

If your event is open and allows guests to invite others, you should encourage that behavior if you want word of the event to spread. Send messages to those guests who are attending urging them to invite friends and help spread the word. You can also send messages specifically to those who have not yet replied to the invitation or to those who have indicated that they may attend urging them to come to the event. For open events, guests can click the Share button to share a link to the Event page on their newsfeed. You can also use the Messaging feature to pass along information about the event, such as changes in the plans or venue rules.

> You can send messages to invitees by clicking the Message Guests link below the event photo on the event's page.

> Remember to monitor your Event page regularly to keep track of Wall postings and respond to queries.

Related Questions

➤ 46. What are the different types of Facebook pages? **Page 133**

➤ 79. What is a "Tweet-up?" **Page 220**

➤ 80. How do I use event-planning websites? **Page 222**

➤ 81. What are tips to hosting a successful event? **Page 224**

Action Item

➤ Set up an event, any event around your brand or the subject you're interested in, and invite at least five friends.

Importance

54. What Does Tagging Do?

A way to identify people in photos is by using the handy tagging feature. To tag someone in a photo is quite easy. You simply go to the Photos page and click the Edit Album link of the album that you want to tag. After you locate a person's face in the photo, you then select the appropriate name in the box that pops up. If the name is not in the box, you can type it out in the text field. If you need to tag yourself, select Me. Repeat this process for everyone in the photo that you would like to tag. When you finish, click Save Changes.

When you tag a friend in a photo, anyone can see more images of the friend by clicking the View Photos Of link beneath that person's profile picture. The feature enables you to go a step further to tag someone else's photos while browsing through them. To do this, from the actions listed under the photo, click Tag This Photo.

To remove a tag from a photo that someone else has uploaded and tagged you in, simply view the photo, and then choose Remove Tag at the bottom next to your name. The photo will no longer be linked to your profile.

Another tagging feature Facebook offers is the ability to tag someone in a status update. The @mentions tagging feature enables people to stay updated on information relevant to them without having to browse everyone's photos and posts every day. This enhances your ability to stay engaged, connected, and updated. The @mentions tagging feature is extremely simple to use, and if you are familiar with the feature in Twitter that does the same thing, you already know how to use it.

To use the @mentions tagging feature, place the @symbol before the name of the person or brand. A drop-down menu appears and offers you options based on what you typed. Then when you finish creating your update, post it.

Next, not only does it appear on your profile as a hyperlink to the mentioned page, it also shows up on the person or brand's Wall. In other words, if you tag it, it will be notified. This way nobody misses things that apply to them. Of course, if they do not want to be mentioned in your status, or do not want others to connect to them through your posting, they have the ability to remove the tag from your post; this helps protect their privacy. Therefore, when someone happens upon your

> You can set the Notifications setting to alert you when someone tags you or even one of your photos.

> If you tag a person in a photo that you did not upload, you cannot remove or edit the tag. Only the owner of the photo and the tagged user can do that.

status update, post, or picture, they can click the link and it takes them to the person's profile or Event page and gives them more information about the person, place, or event mentioned.

The great thing about the @mentions tagging feature is that, in theory, it means you no longer miss things that involve you. Status updates and other Wall posts become more meaningful because the people involved are hyperlinked.

Related Questions

➔ 56. How do I reach out to other brands on Facebook? **Page 158**

➔ 67. How can I share pictures? **Page 187**

➔ 97. How can I build influence? **Page 258**

➔ 98. How can I keep my social media efforts interesting? **Page 261**

Action Item

➔ Go through one of your Facebook photo albums and start tagging!

Importance

55. What Are Facebook Lists?

Facebook came out with a way to filter your friends so that you can better target updates and improve your security settings for the various types of content that you put on your personal page. This can be particularly useful if you have many different types of contacts that blur the line between personal connections and professional connections.

Under Facebook's privacy settings, you can select which lists or individuals can or cannot access the varying information. How you filter these settings will be based on what you feel comfortable with and what types of content usually find their way onto your page.

If you have many friends from college connected to your account, but also have a lot of business associates, you may want to consider that photos posted on your page by others are only viewable by college friends. That will reduce the risk of colleagues seeing pictures of last weekend's escapades. Also, if you have a lot of family connected, controlling those photos may help to prevent your friends and colleagues from being able to see images for you in funny situations from your childhood (like that picture of you on the toilet when you first got potty-trained)!

Friend lists can be created by going to the Friends page, clicking Edit Friends at the top of the page, and then clicking Create New List. You can add people to the list by searching through your friends and selecting them using the checkboxes. If you are editing an existing list, you can hover over the name and a button that says Edit Lists will appear next to the friend. You can then select or de-select the lists you want that particular friend to appear in.

Rule of Thumb   When you filter privacy settings, try to not completely block everything from a certain list. If you're doing so, you may want to reconsider approving those friendship requests in the first place.

Related Questions

➡ 5. What is my brand's objective? **Page 18**

➡ 91. How do I figure out who my key influencers are? **Page 248**

➡ 97. How can I build influence? **Page 258**

➡ 99. How do I keep from being overwhelmed? **Page 263**

Action Item

➡ Create a list for "Family" and add all of your friends who are family members to that list. Repeat this for every other group you want to have as a segment of your friends list.

Importance

56. How Do I Reach Out to Other Brands on Facebook?

Facebook has made it easier for brands to communicate on Facebook. Previously, a personal user was more connected to a business Page because in order to comment on other brand Pages, personal users had to "like" the other brand, and then write something on their own brand Page that referenced the targeted page by using the at (@) symbol. When the at symbol was used, a drop-down menu would appear that filtered in real time based on the letters typed in immediately after.

Instead of going through this sometimes arduous process, users can now switch to using Facebook as a Page rather than as a person. Comments can be written directly on another brand's Page, but only after the brand has liked that Page.

Rule of Thumb   Commenting on other brand Pages should be done with care. You don't want to look like you're spamming other Pages or you'll ruin the credibility of your brand and upset other users.

Related Questions

➡ 54. What does tagging do? **Page 154**

➡ 64. What sites can help me find relevant news? **Page 176**

➡ 94. What do I include as my next steps? **Page 252**

➡ 97. How can I build influence? **Page 258**

Action Item

➡ Acting as your Page, like another brand Page and make a comment if appropriate.

57. Should I Link My Facebook and Twitter Accounts?

Importance

Facebook allows users to automatically push Facebook Page updates to Twitter. This practice is commonly debated, because automation can sometimes curb actual conversation. Also, Facebook allows much more content than Twitter in a given update and will often get cut off on Twitter.

When deciding whether or not to automate your Facebook feed to Twitter, consider what benefits will arise from this practice. One immediate benefit that is often enticing enough to convince users to link the two accounts is that it will help to reduce the amount of time you need to set aside for pushing content out. However, you still have to check both accounts to see if anyone has responded.

The problem with linking the two accounts is that the typical user on Twitter is often very different from the typical Facebooker. Twitter users are accustomed to rapid updates in short bursts of activity. Facebook users tend to converse more and have longer comments or questions. Because of this difference in content expectation, it's usually better to have different types of content for your varying audiences.

An easy way to deal with content control and time management is to use a third-party updating service that allows you to use multiple accounts within their service. Web-based tools like Hootsuite.com, or desktop applications like Seesmic or Tweetdeck, allow users to set up different types of accounts like Twitter, Facebook, LinkedIn, and even Foursquare, so that all updates for all accounts can be made from one central place.

Rule of Thumb   Use third-party tools to benefit from displaying analytics so that you can track your ROI.

Related Questions

➤ 6. Who is my target audience? **Page 20**

➤ 13. How do I choose which sites to use? **Page 52**

➤ 22. What can I install on my website to encourage conversations? **Page 75**

➤ 99. How do I keep from being overwhelmed? **Page 263**

Action Item

➤ Skip syncing your Facebook and Twitter accounts. If you want to make it easier to post to both, set up a third-party tool like Hootsuite for posting to multiple profiles at once rather than having one service feed to another.

Chapter 8
LinkedIn

In this chapter:

Importance

58. What Is LinkedIn?

LinkedIn is a little different than other social networking sites discussed in this book. This site is set up for business professionals. Therefore, members are more formal in their interactions. With LinkedIn, you find less casual conversations and more conversations about business.

In 2002, five people got together and created LinkedIn. Reid Hoffman, Allen Blue, Jean-Luc Vaillant, Eric Ly, and Konstantin Guericke had the vision to create a social networking site to enable professionals to connect with the goal to advance their businesses and professional relationships. The overall goal of the site is to enable users to maintain connections with people they know and trust in business.

The mission statement is "To connect the world's professionals to make them more productive and successful." LinkedIn achieves this mission with many different features and tools such as:

> LinkedIn is set up for the business professional; therefore, people act in a much more professional manner on the site.

- ➤ A network that consists of direct connections (first-degree connections), the connections of each of their connections (second-degree connections) and also the connections of second-degree connections (third-degree connections). This can be used to gain an introduction to someone a person wants to know through a mutual, trusted contact.

- ➤ A way to find jobs, people, and business opportunities recommended by someone in one's contact network.

- ➤ A way to hire through employers who can list jobs and search for potential candidates.

- ➤ A way to review the profile of hiring managers and discover which of their existing contacts can introduce job seekers to them.

- ➤ A way to post photos and view photos of others to aid in identification.

- ➤ A method for following different companies and receive notifications when employees have joined, left, or have been promoted within the business.

- ➤ A way for users to save jobs they would like to apply for.

LinkedIn uses the *gated-access approach* in which contact with any professional requires either a pre-existing relationship or a mutual contact to introduce them. This is intended to build trust among the service's users.

LinkedIn also enables users to research companies with which they might be interested in working. When typing the name of a given company in the search box, statistics about the company are provided. These might include the ratio of female to male employees, the percentage of the most common titles/positions held within the company, the location of the company's headquarters and offices, or a list of present and former employees.

LinkedIn's Answers feature is a powerful tool that enables users to ask questions for the community to answer. This feature is free, the questions are potentially more business-oriented, and the identity of the people asking and answering questions is known. This is discussed in detail later.

 Related Questions

➡ 2. Brand, Online Presence—What's the difference? **Page 4**

➡ 12. What social networks best fit my goals? **Page 40**

➡ 64. What sites can help me find relevant news? **Page 176**

➡ 73. How do I track what is said about my brand? **Page 202**

Action Item

➡ Follow the steps that LinkedIn provides you until your profile is marked as 100 percent complete.

Importance

59. How Do I Use LinkedIn?

Setting up an account on the site is easy, but it takes a lot more time than most social networking sites (see Figure 8-1). This is because you enter a lot of your past and current work experience, but doing so can have a higher return for the business professional.

To join LinkedIn, sign up below ... it's free!

First Name:	
Last Name:	
Email:	
New Password:	

6 or more characters

Join LinkedIn *

Already on LinkedIn? Sign in

LinkedIn helps you...

→ Establish your professional profile online
→ Stay in touch with colleagues and friends
→ Find experts, ideas and opportunities

* By clicking Join LinkedIn, you are indicating that you have read, understood, and agree to LinkedIn's User Agreement and Privacy Policy

LinkedIn Corporation © 2011 | Commercial use of this site without express authorization is prohibited.

FIGURE 8-1: LinkedIn makes it easy to open an account.

After completing the fields with your first name, last name, email, and password, LinkedIn asks you for professional information to start building your profile.

LinkedIn makes it easy to add and update your information. (See Figure 8-2.) You simply click the Add button and complete the fields. Another way the site makes it easy is if you have a completed resume, you can import it into LinkedIn and make any corrections as needed.

Dean, Let's get your professional profile started

I am currently:	Employed
* Country:	United States
* ZIP Code:	
	e.g. 94043 (Only your region will be public, not your ZIP code)
* Company:	
* Job Title:	

Create my profile

* Indicates required field.

A LinkedIn profile helps you...

→ Showcase your skills and experience
→ Be found for new opportunities
→ Stay in touch with colleagues and friends

LinkedIn Corporation © 2011 | Commercial use of this site without express authorization is prohibited.

FIGURE 8-2: LinkedIn has an intuitive site and makes it easy to add and update information.

Rule of Thumb   Always proofread all information before posting. Typos make a bad impression.

As you build out your profile, a handy profile completeness bar updates, letting you know how far you are from having a 100% completed profile.

Make sure you have included a picture to your profile, checked spelling, and placed links to your personal website and other social networks.

After you create a profile, you can start networking by clicking the Add Connections button. LinkedIn realizes this is the backbone of its site, so this button can always be found in the top-right corner of the site, regardless of what page you are on.

Clicking Add Connections enables you to scan your email contacts to find out who else you have communicated with is on the site. You can get a list of people; some have the LinkedIn logo to the right of their names. These are the people you should invite to connect. The logo means that they have an account set up on the network. Those without the logo will get an invite asking them to sign up on LinkedIn. I do not personally recommend inviting those not on the site because the invitations are considered "spammy" (see Figure 8-3).

FIGURE 8-3: Add only people you know as connections and make sure they're business-related contacts.

One thing to be aware of when inviting people to connect is that you actually know them. Now you might think, "Well of course I know them; I have their emails in my contacts." That is not always the case. If you are carbon copied on emails or email services such as Gmail, save those. If you ask to connect with those people and they decline because they do not know who you are, they may report you. If you are reported too many times, LinkedIn will suspend your account.

> **Rule of Thumb**   Use LinkedIn to connect with employers, fellow employees, and friends with the professional purpose of finding jobs, people, and business opportunities—not to share your personal social life.

As LinkedIn is considered a site for the business professional, most users interact in that way. They do not share pictures of their cats, talk about what they had for dinner, or who they are dating. Unlike other social network sites, there is less status updating. Those who do update their status do it mostly around work-related topics. LinkedIn has an option to link a Twitter account to your LinkedIn status update. As discussed in the in Chapter 6, Twitter is for more casual conversations. Casual conversations on LinkedIn are discouraged because users might find it inappropriate for the site.

> **Rule of Thumb**   Use a picture of yourself as your profile picture. You would be amazed at the number of people who use their business logos or pictures of their cats or an image of Bart Simpson.

Some other things you should not do include the following:

- Do not become an invitation spammer. You may want to connect with every Ed, Craig, and Roman out there but trying to do so is just annoying.

- Do not put anything in the name field other than your name.

- Do not send an invitation without saying why you want to connect.

- Do not forward introductions that seem iffy. If you are connected to high profile people, I would not make introductions all the time. You will lose some of your credibility along the way.

- Don't post that you're looking for work if you are connected to your boss.

Rule of Thumb   Remember to keep your profile current and have a profile picture of yourself that was taken in the last year or so... not when you were 12.

Related Questions

➜   4. How do I develop my brand strategy? **Page 13**

➜   64. What sites can help me find relevant news? **Page 176**

➜   76. Do I still need a business card? **Page 214**

➜   88. What does a social media strategy look like? **Page 244**

Action Item

➜   Connect to your real-life friends. The first thing you should do after creating an "amazing" profile is to connect with all your fellow colleagues, past and present. Yes, even the weird guy by the copy machine.

Importance

60. How Do I Get Recommendations?

A powerful feature of LinkedIn is the Recommendations feature. In the past, when you applied for a job, you submitted a resume and several letters of recommendations. Now with LinkedIn Recommendations, you do not need to directly solicit these letters.

> Use the Recommendations feature in the same way as you would a "real-life" letter of recommendation.

Within your profile there is the Recommendations section. These are endorsements from people who may have been a client, colleague, or employer. These add to your online profile by enriching it and adding more information about who you are and what you brought to that position. The fact that someone was willing to take the time to write a recommendation about you shows something about your character (see Figure 8-4).

Some things to keep in mind about recommendations:

➡ When requesting a recommendation, give the person some guidance on what to write about you. You can write something with keywords you are looking for, a specific project, or a client. Some help like this can increase the odds you get the recommendation.

➡ Let the person know the recommendation does not need to be the typical long letter. Just a short paragraph gets the job done.

➡ Keep the number of recommendations you have at a realistic number. You do not want to have 200 recommendations. A potential employer will not look at all 200, and the best ones will get lost and have little impact. A good number is anywhere from 10 to 30.

To get someone to write a recommendation for you, start by clicking the Recommendations button on your profile. This brings you to the Recommendation section of your profile.

Then click Ask for a Recommendation. Then click the Request Recommendations tab at the top of page. You then have three simple steps to complete:

1. Choose what position you would like the recommendation for.

2. Choose who you want to ask for a recommendation.

3. Add the messages you want to include to the person you ask for the recommendation.

> "Ed's extremely reliable, detail oriented, very personable, always responsive, and operates with unquestioned integrity. He's a great guy to work with, and I'd never hesitate to work with him again, anytime." *July 29, 2008*
>
> **Top qualities:** Great Results, Expert, High Integrity
>
> (2nd) Paul D'Anna,
> hired Ed as a Real Estate Agent in 2006

> "Ed is a well-organized, detail-oriented, trustworthy person. He successfully assisted me in the purchase of my first home." *June 13, 2008*
>
> **Top qualities:** Personable, Expert, High Integrity
>
> (2nd) Debbie Sullivan,
> hired Ed as a Real Estate Agent in 2006

> "Ed provides an invaluable service to his clients. He maintains a high level of trust and integrity. He never loses sight of the fact that he is there to advocate for his clients and help navigate the real estate waters. I refer as much business as I can to Ed, as I am totally confident that he will always exceed the expectations!" *March 20, 2008*
>
> (2nd) Christine Quinn, *Escrow Officer, Financial Title Company*
> was a consultant or contractor to Ed at Intero Real Estate Services

FIGURE 8-4: Recommendations can make a great impression for potential employers.

Rule of Thumb   Personalize your request for a recommendation and offer to provide a recommendation in return.

LinkedIn has a canned request message but strongly consider personalizing the request. Let the person know why you are asking them specifically for this endorsement. Also, offer to give them a recommendation in return. This method can give you the highest odds to get a person to recommend you.

Related Questions

➔ 12. What social networks best fit my goals? **Page 40**

➔ 19. What pages are essential for my website? **Page 68**

➔ 97. How can I build influence? **Page 258**

➔ 98. How do I keep from being overwhelmed? **Page 261**

> You may not want to ask your current employer, your past employer, and all your friends for a recommendation at the same time. It may look like you're looking for a new job...your boss might not be happy!

Action Item

➔ Find three people you know WELL and ask for recommendations on a project or job you have had together.

Importance

61. What Is LinkedIn Answers?

LinkedIn has a feature that is quite likely one of the most underused and overlooked in a professional social networking strategy. At first glance, LinkedIn Answers is a simple tool; you post a question and get an answer. There is a lot more to it than that.

LinkedIn Answers consists of two things: asking questions and answering questions. Even though it seems like a very simplistic idea, answering questions posted on LinkedIn Answers actually reinforces your position as a thought leader or industry expert, thus helping you expand your network and showcase your expertise (see Figure 8-5).

> **?** **What are your recommendations for must-read sources for the latest news and trends in brand marketing?**
> 4 answers | Asked by Bryan Person (1st) | 5 months ago in Business Development
>
> **?** **Do you have any business success stories that you can directly attribute to LinkedIn?**
> 16 answers | Asked by Rick Itzkowich (1st) | 7 months ago in Business Development
>
> **?** **How have you used social networks to crowdsource opinions, feedback or input from many others? (like LinkedIn Answers!)**
> 13 answers | Asked by Aliza Sherman Risdahl (1st) | 8 months ago in Business Development, Market Research and Definition
>
> **?** **Writing some articles that are due for American Express OPENForum. I write about marketing, business growth, entrepreneur stuff. What kinds of topics do you wish I'd cover?**
> 27 answers | Asked by Chris Brogan (1st) | 8 months ago in Business Development
>
> **?** **Must tell truth. What is your leading motivation for answering questions/creating discussions on LI?**
> 23 answers | Asked by Lisa Radin (1st) | March 4, 2010 in Business Development

FIGURE 8-5: LinkedIn Answers is a great way to network.

To start, click the Answers section at the top of the site. It takes you to the Answers Home section of LinkedIn. There you can ask a question about anything in your field of work or something in a totally different field you want to find out about.

Following is what is so great about Answers:

→ You can easily and quickly ask a question about something in your field. This question can be sorted into your specific business categories. People will begin answering the question or referring you to people/places to find an answer. As this happens you begin networking and chatting with other professionals.

➔ You can answer questions about subjects in your field. By doing this you begin to build up a network of people who see you as a thought leader in your field.

➔ When you answer a question, it can be marked Best Answer. This happens when the person who asks the question believes your answer to be the best. This adds to building you up as a thought leader.

Related Questions

➔ 5. What is my brand's objective? **Page 18**

➔ 90. What are key influencers? **Page 247**

➔ 95. How often should I update my strategy? **Page 254**

➔ 98. How can I keep my social media efforts interesting? **Page 261**

Action Item

➔ Check out questions being asked in your groups or within your network. Answer one to the best of your professional ability. Make sure you do not include a request to visit your profile in your answer! Your answers should be used to build your credibility, not drive traffic through requests.

Importance

62. What Are Contacts and Can I Have Too Many?

As you begin to add contacts and start to network on the site, you see your number of connections starts to increase. This number increases until it hits 500. The displayed number of connections will never show more than 500. Yet, you can have an unlimited number of connections on the site. LinkedIn wants to discourage people from building up a large, unreasonable amount of connections made up of people that they do not know.

 Related Questions

➜ 40. What is the difference between "followers" and "following?" **Page 115**

➜ 52. How do Facebook "likes" help me? **Page 150**

➜ 58. What is LinkedIn? **Page 162**

➜ 99. How do I keep from being overwhelmed? **Page 263**

Action Item

➜ Remember those emails you added in contacts? Time to add them to your LinkedIn network.

63. What Are LinkedIn Groups?

Importance

LinkedIn Groups enable its members to join a smaller network of connections within the site. At the top of the home page, members can click the Groups tab. Then a drop-down menu displays several options including Group Directory. When you click Group Directory, you can pick a group that represents your industry or area of interest (see Figure 8-6). Think of these groups as a special areas on the site that enable you to talk about things you find of interest; they are niche areas for people with common interests.

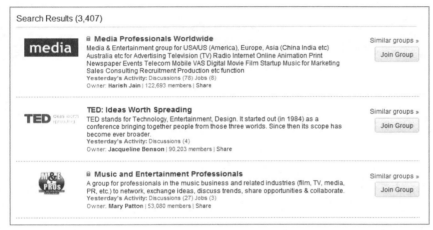

FIGURE 8-6: Join groups relevant to your profession and professional interests.

There are several reasons to join groups:

➔ Building relationships with your industry peers

➔ Sharing information, practices, tips, and tricks

➔ Exchanging knowledge and challenging timely discussions

➔ Finding and posting jobs

➔ Developing possible partnerships

Rule of Thumb LinkedIn Answers and Groups are excellent ways to network, build relationships, and exchange information.

Beware that when you join a group, a badge is displayed on your profile page. So, you may not want to join that "Justin Beiber 4-Ever" group.

Related Questions

➤ 10. How do I brand my online identity? **Page 34**

➤ 12. What social networks best fit my goals? **Page 40**

➤ 78. How do I find (and get) speaking engagements? **Page 218**

➤ 97. How can I build influence? **Page 258**

Action Item

➤ Find a group in your niche and ask to join it. Look for one that has a lot of members, not a group with just one or two.

Other Key Social Media Websites

Importance

64. What Sites Can Help Me Find Relevant News?

The most successful social media campaigns usually come from brands that don't just create a lot of noise. If a brand jumped right in to offering specials and deals and contests from Day 1, that brand sets an expectation in its followers that this is the type of content they can expect to find moving forward. If this isn't what your brand is about, there needs to be more meat to your content than just self-serving updates and contests.

Some brands choose to include news from other sources to build their social presence. This can be current events, posts from relevant blogs, tips and tricks or just information that may be interesting to the target market.

There are sites and mobile applications that can work to help gather relevant news and information. Using these sites, you can more easily filter through various topics to quickly find content that can help build your brand presence and establish a good foundation for your social media campaign.

Alltop

Alltop is self-billed as an "online magazine rack of the web." This site aggregates headlines and puts them all in one place, sorted by topic and source. The headlines are links that go directly to the original article. Users of the site can create their own Alltop page and handpick content sources (see Figure 9-1). Visiting a personalized Alltop page is like being able to place all of your favorite newspapers on your desk with all the articles you like placed on the front page.

Blogs can be submitted to Alltop for inclusion on the site, but they are vetted before they are included. The name of the site is Alltop because the content included is supposed to be all the "top news" on the web. This control is necessary to ensure that site maintains its high levels of quality.

The order of page content varies. No real details about the order is available on the site, but lack of user input, like ratings or voting, do hint that it doesn't always have to do with popularity.

FIGURE 9-1: You can personalize an Alltop page to display all the feeds that interest you.

Digg

Digg is similar to Alltop in that it collects news headlines and sorts them by topic. The major difference is that users can influence visibility of a particular headline by "digging" stories that they find interesting, newsworthy, funny, or generally useful.

Another major difference is that users don't have to visit Digg.com in order to rate stories. Any article or page anywhere on the web can have a Digg button, which automatically updates that article's presence on Digg.com. The idea is that the "community," meaning users of the web in general, "diggs" articles as they read them. The more diggs an article gets, the higher the placement and visibility on Digg.com.

Every article has the potential of landing on the Digg home page, which theoretically will generate high amounts of web traffic for the article source. Using the community-based ranking system, Digg is essentially motivating content creators to write more thoughtful, useful pieces.

Don't try to game (or try to trick) the system though; there are various rules and restrictions in place that help the site regulate the voting to avoid issues like spamming.

There are eight top-level categories, within which there are between five and ten subcategories:

> Theoretically, Digg's page should contain a list of the best content from all around the Internet. In reality, this doesn't always happen because of people who do try (and succeed) to trick the system.

- ➤ Technology
- ➤ World and Business
- ➤ Science
- ➤ Gaming
- ➤ Lifestyle
- ➤ Entertainment
- ➤ Sports
- ➤ Offbeat

Flipboard

This "personalized social magazine" is developed exclusively for the iPad at the time of this publication (see Figure 9-2). It uses your Twitter and Facebook accounts to put together an electronic magazine of the news and updates happening on your feeds. To help filter content further, Flipboard categorizes and sorts based on topic and your interaction.

FIGURE 9-2: Flipboard is known for its beautiful interface.

Zite

Another iPad-specific application, Zite is also billed as a personalized magazine. Content is synced with a user's Twitter account, but can also be pulled in from blogs that are placed in a Google Reader account. As stories are read, Zite essentially records what you seem to like, and then reconfigures to intelligently filter and sort based on your interests.

Other Options

Services like the ones listed previously are all basically designed to do one thing: help filter information on the web so that users can more easily find content to consume and distribute via the various social channels. By using these services, you can efficiently find information that can be used to help establish your brand as a topical "expert" or key resource for others. A brand with a reputation for consistently and thoroughly understanding its industry is often one that users will gravitate to more, making the return on investment in a social media campaign more likely to be successful.

Related Questions

Action Item

➜   Make a list of the websites you currently gather your news from. See if they use RSS feeds, so that you can pull all the news sources together in one place. Using one of the web or mobile-based applications for social bookmarking, set up a private feed for yourself to start a library of useful content. Even if you don't use this as part of your campaign later, you'll have a central source to collect information you need about your particular interest.

65. What Is Social Bookmarking?

Importance

Like folding down the corners of a book, bookmarking allows you to save websites or pages to your web browser so that you can view them later. Social bookmarking takes this one step further by saving your bookmarked sites in a public fashion, so that other users can both contribute to and gain insight from the collective effort that gets put into building resources relating to specific topics.

Social bookmarking originated with a website called Delicious. The service that this site provided brought new light to the usefulness of "crowd-sourced" information. By seeing what other people with related interests find useful, a user can build their virtual library while gaining a better understanding of what their target audience is most interested in reading about.

Social media campaigns that incorporate social bookmarking focus on developing the "thought leadership" aspect of a brand. This is positive for brands that require consumer loyalty.

StumbleUpon is the channel-surfing tool of the Internet, with millions of users. It enables people to quickly and easily visit and discover new web pages that they would more than likely never come across.

To use StumbleUpon, you install a toolbar add-on to your web browser, sign up, pick topics that interest you, and press the Stumble button. Topics can range from photography, games, web development, humor, family, or any of the hundreds of other subjects.

Over time, as you rate pages, StumbleUpon learns what you like and matches you with similar Stumblers, giving you pages that they've marked as "thumbs up." You'll end up finding amusing, interesting sites that you otherwise would have never even thought of looking for.

How It Works

StumbleUpon gets to know what you like when you rate web pages and matches you up with similar users. Additionally, when you add new quality sites, you start getting good "Karma," and future sites that you submit and your votes will have more weight.

Adding a site is easy: Just give a page a thumbs up that hasn't been stumbled yet, and it'll be added to the database and you'll get credit for it.

How to Make StumbleUpon Benefit Your Site

Stumble your own pages. There's nothing against the code of Stumble-Upon that says that you can't Stumble your own pages. However, you have to choose content that will attract Stumblers' attention and keep them on the site for longer than a few seconds.

Related Questions

→ 7. Am I reflecting my brand? **Page 22**

→ 12. What social networks best fit my goals? **Page 40**

→ 24. What do I write about? **Page 83**

→ 72. How can I use social media to help my SEO? **Page 199**

> The ease of Stumbling also leads to one of the downsides of Stumble-Upon; it makes it easy for users to leave sites right after pressing the button because the site is bookmarked to view at a later time. Make sure that your content is compelling so that us-ers are more motivated to remember that they want to view your site in more detail later. Make the first impression strong.

Action Item

→ Go through the websites you currently have bookmarked in your browser. Clean out the bookmarks that don't positively affect your brand, and then move them over into a social bookmarking service to jump-start your presence.

66. What Are the Best Sites for Video Sharing?

Importance

Videos are quickly becoming popular content to share online. As people continue to turn more to the Internet for both information and entertainment, videos serve to satisfy both of those needs. Video-hosting sites are popular tools for content creators because of the ease in social sharing.

Sites like YouTube and Vimeo are sharing services that allow users to create their own personal channel. These channels act as a place for users to hold multiple videos, and they can be made either private or public depending on the users' needs.

A brand can develop presence on YouTube or Vimeo by either uploading content or responding to other content. People who view the videos can rate the quality of the video and write comments. Videos with high popularity can be pushed to the top of the service's recommendation engine, creating greater likelihood of visibility. As videos are viewed, YouTube and Vimeo place related or recommended videos in a sidebar for user consideration.

YouTube was created by three friends from PayPal: Chad Hurley, Steve Chen, and Jawed Karim, who raised $3.5 million in venture capital to launch their open exchange video site in February 2005. Less than two years later, Google bought YouTube for $1.65 billion.

The concept is simple. People post videos on YouTube and watch and comment on the videos others have posted. The videos can be anything from a simple rant into a cell phone camera by a frustrated teenager to a favorite sports clips and everything in between. The numbers generated by YouTube are mind blowing: One hundred million videos are on the YouTube servers, with 65,000 new ones uploaded every day. They're watched by 20 million viewers a month.

Comedian Judson Laipply's 6-minute "Evolution of Dance," an entertaining journey through the history of dance styles, is the all-time most-popular video on YouTube with close to 41 million hits. It earned Laipply appearances on *Good Morning America* and a dozen other national television outlets.

Another clip posted on YouTube in November 2010 showed the arrest of alleged gang member William Cardenas, triggering an FBI investigation into police brutality. In May 2006, the Lonelygirl15 video diaries appeared on YouTube, chronicling the small-town life of an American teenager named Bree. The series became wildly popular, but a few months later, it was discovered that Bree was actually an actress from New Zealand who was hired by two guys from California to pull off an elaborate publicity stunt.

Rebecca Black, a 13-year-old aspiring singer, was the subject of what numerous media outlets (including the Huffington Post and Yahoo Music) were dubbing a viral Internet sensation...and not in a positive way. This video of Black's song Friday, garnered over 2.2 million views in less than a weekend. Over 2% of viewers gave the video negative feedback, making it YouTube's "most hated video" according to the online blog Mashable.

There are dozens of others like these who have found instant Internet celebrity by dancing, singing, mixing Mentos with Coke, posting odd video resumes, and in any number of other creative ways. That is part of the YouTube phenomenon. Its simplicity and global reach—and its youthful demographics—are driving and changing traditional news media and entertainment, and even business and politics.

To join the YouTube community, go to the sign-up page at YouTube, choose a username and password, and enter your basic information. Then click the Sign Up button, and you're in. Browsing the millions of videos available is simple. After creating a free account, you can browse through 12 categories, search by keyword, or simply check out what's popular that day. If you like one particular video, you can subscribe to that user's future videos, using clear prompts on every new page.

Uploading your own video is almost as simple. In the upper-right corner of a YouTube page, click Upload Videos, and enter as much information as you want. Click Go Upload a File, locate the file on your hard drive, and then click Upload Video. YouTube does not allow any video that portrays graphic sex and violence. Those that do are quickly flagged and taken down; so are any that proffer hatred or other potentially offensive material.

Although YouTube is an open exchange, you can make your videos available only to a small group of family, friends, or business associates. Either choose between Private or Public when you first upload, or, after uploading your video, click Edit Video Info, scroll down to the Broadcast section, and select Private.

YouTube is a true global community, with numerous user groups and contests to encourage users to create their own videos, reachable through the Community button on any page. The contests might focus on ways to spend a tax refund, telling your darkest secrets, or creating a new music video. Some have large cash prizes.

YouTube discourages users from downloading videos to their own computers, preferring that they watch videos online. However, you may embed videos on your own website. Copy the code from the embed box found under About this Video on the right while the video plays. Copy the code, then paste it into your website or blog to embed it.

Videos uploaded to YouTube (see Figure 9-3) must be less than 15 minutes in length. There is also a limit of 2 GB for the size of the uploaded file. High-definition videos are accepted, as long as they meet the other requirements.

Even if you don't have videos to share, creating a channel to collect the videos that you believe your audience will find useful may be just as positive for your brand as having your own to publish.

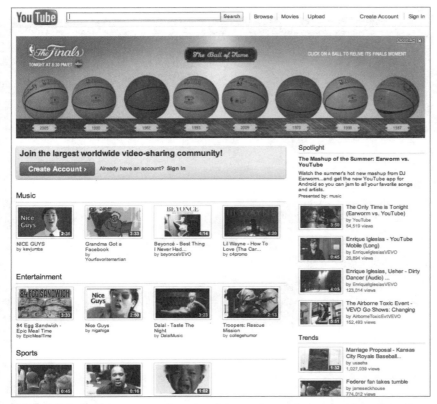

FIGURE 9-3: YouTube is a popular network for posting and viewing videos. Stars like Justin Bieber were discovered on YouTube.

Vimeo limits uploads to 500 MB per week, but offers uploads of HD videos of up to 5 GB as a premium option.

Alternatively, live broadcasts may be more beneficial to a brand. Services like Ustream offer the ability for users to create content and stream, or broadcast, live using a Ustream channel and then allow the audience to interact before, during, and after the broadcast, incorporating social tools like Facebook or Twitter to continue the conversations.

The decision to use video or stream in a social media campaign or to help grow a brand presence should be made by determining the needs of the target audience and whether those needs are met best by written content or recorded. Videos can be aesthetically pleasing and useful, but if not created to satisfy the needs of a particular audience, they can also easily deter people from the content and result in an unsuccessful campaign.

 Related Questions

➤ 12. What social networks best fit my goals? **Page 40**

➤ 13. How do I choose which sites to use? **Page 52**

➤ 38. What should I do if I don't want a blog? **Page 110**

➤ 98. How can I keep my social media efforts interesting? **Page 261**

Action Item

➤ Sign up for one of the video services and either upload a video or start subscribing to relevant content creators.

67. How Can I Share Pictures?

Importance

Pictures add color to a website and instant interest to a Twitter feed or Facebook page. If the campaign is more specific to photos, there are other sites that can help to promote a brand's presence. Sites like Flickr, Photobucket, and Picasa have established full-fledged photo-sharing communities where a brand can grow its reputation as a photography powerhouse.

Mobile phone cameras are becoming increasingly sophisticated, and with that, mobile photography applications are rapidly being developed and integrated into the social community. These applications, such as Instagram, Incredibooth, Path, and Hipstamatic, provide a way for an average person to basically become an instant photographer. If photos are important to a campaign and mobile is the medium that proves most efficient and practical, applications like these will be useful for a brand.

Facebook and other social networks also offer the tools to upload pictures directly. Twitter, at this time, requires the use of other tools to take advantage of photo sharing, but third-party applications like Hootsuite, Tweetdeck, or Seesmic can show the photos within the tweet. Twitpic will allow you to link images to tweets (see Figure 9-4). Twitter announced in June, 2011 that it would adopt photo sharing for use within the system. At the time of this writing, the service had not yet rolled out.

Before using photographs as content for your brand's social media efforts, consider the quality of photos that you will be able to provide to users as well as the context in which you provide them. Although photos of a city skyline on a sunny day may be pleasing to look at, they won't necessarily help build your brand's social presence unless the core product or service offering has to do with something like the weather. For restaurants or retailers, photos of the day's special products is content that can entice potential consumers to buy. As with any other type of content, the measurement of the success the photographs contribute to a social media campaign is gauged by the relevancy of the subject matter.

> Some brands use services like Flickr to collect other brand submissions. This becomes a sort of crowd-sourced portfolio, showcasing your work amongst what others include so that they can see what your brand has to offer.

FIGURE 9-4: Twitpic is a popular service that people can use to link images to tweets.

 **Related Questions**

➧ 12. What social networks best fit my goals? **Page 40**

➧ 13. How do I choose which sites to use? **Page 52**

➧ 38. What should I do if I don't want a blog? **Page 110**

➧ 98. How can I keep my social media efforts interesting? **Page 261**

Action Item

➧ If you have a portfolio or other images that will support your
brand, upload them to a service like Flickr.

Chapter 10
Getting Found Online

In this chapter:

Importance

68. What Is SEO?

Search Engine Optimization (SEO) is the process to make a website or page more "readable" by search engines. The desired result of these efforts is for the website to appear at or near the top of search results in a search engine. The higher a website ranks in the results of a search, the greater the chance that the site will be visited by users. It is common practice for Internet users to not click through pages and pages of search results. Most people click somewhere on the first few pages of these results. Where a website ranks in a search is essential for directing more traffic toward the site. SEO helps to improve the chances that the search engine can find a site.

SEO efforts typically start with submitting a website to search engines. Although search engines do crawl through most websites, submitting a website to the engine directories helps ensure that the website can be found and indexed more quickly. As with most services, search engine submissions are usually free, but some engines require fees. Determining which search engines to submit a website to will depend on the requirements of the website and the desired results from the SEO efforts.

Other efforts in the process to optimize a website for strong search engine results include tailoring content to be specific to the anticipated search engine queries and properly coding a website to be clean, concise, and semantic.

There are hundreds of books on SEO—maybe even thousands. Following is a list of some ways to improve your SEO efforts:

➤ Content is king, so be sure to have good, well-written, fresh, and unique content that focuses on your primary keyword or keyword phrase.

➤ If content is king, then links are queen. Build a network of quality backlinks using your keyword phrase as the link. Remember, if there isn't a good, logical reason for that site to link to you, you don't want the link.

➤ Don't be obsessed with page rank. It is just a small part of the ranking algorithm. A site with a lower page rank can actually outrank one with a higher page rank.

The most widely used search engines are Google and Bing. Always include these sites in your optimization efforts by going to each search engine and submitting your site using their respective processes. As a key piece to most Internet marketing strategies, SEO helps to improve the visibility of a website on search engine sites such as Google, Yahoo, and Bing, which can result in increased organic web traffic (see Figure 10-1).

Because it doesn't cost anything to be listed in a search engine, and if a brand invests in optimizing its online presence, it can often result in positive return on investment (ROI). The low-to-zero cost means that any action of a web visitor to use or promote your brand after visiting your website will be positive return.

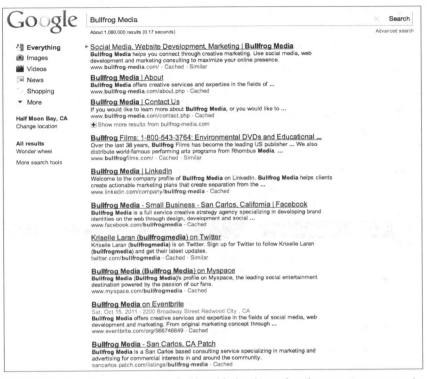

FIGURE 10-1: A Google search for Bullfrog Media shows that the company appears in nine of the top ten links on the first page of search results.

- Be sure you have a unique, keyword-focused Title tag on every page of your site. And if you must have the name of your company in it, put it at the end. Unless you are a major brand name that is a household name, your business name will probably get few searches.

- Focus on search phrases, not single keywords, and put your location in your text (our Palm Springs store, not our store) to help local searches find you.

- If your site content doesn't change often, your site needs a blog because search spiders like fresh text. Blog at least three times a week with good, fresh content to feed those little crawlers.

- Search engines want natural language content. Don't try to stuff your text with keywords. It won't work. Search engines look at how many times a term is in your content and its context.

Do you have a new website you want spidered? Submitting through Google's regular submission form can take weeks. The quickest way to get your site spidered is by getting a link to it through another quality site.

➤ Links from .edu domains are given nice weight by the search engines. Run a search for possible nonprofit .edu sites that are looking for sponsors.

➤ SEO is useless if you have a weak or nonexistent call to action. Make sure your call to action is clear and present.

➤ Links (especially deep links) from a site with high PR are golden. High PR indicates high trust, so the back links can carry more weight.

➤ Add a URL in the address bar so that users can gradually get used to the new URL.

Related Questions

➤ 15. How do I set up a website? **Page 60**

➤ 19. What pages are essential for my website? **Page 68**

➤ 23. How do I add a blog to my website? **Page 82**

➤ 69. What keywords do I use? **Page 193**

Action Item

➤ Install an analytical tool onto your website so that you can track website statistics for use in determining your ROI. A popular tool to use is Google Analytics. It's free!

69. What Keywords Do I Use?

Importance

As general users of the web, people often type in the term or phrase that makes most sense to them when looking for the information. For example, someone looking for a new dentist in San Francisco may type San Francisco dentist into Google's search bar. The websites or information found online (such as Twitter pages, addresses and phone numbers in the Google map directory, news articles, and so on) that Google feels are most relevant to that search term populate into the search results page. Keywords are the terms or phrases that people use to search for a website. The quantity and quality of these terms as used on a website can help search engines to determine the relevance of a website to the keywords. The more relevant a search engine deems the website, the earlier the website can show up in search results.

Research can be done to determine what keywords are most commonly used for a specific site or topic. By using these keywords in relevant context, a website can tailor its content to focus on what the brand believes is most important to its consumers.

Various tools are available to help determine what keywords to use for a website. These tools show the level of demand for each keyword and can assist in ensuring that the selected keywords have the greatest likelihood of positive ROI.

When selecting keywords, it's best to be as specific as possible. The more specific the keyword, the less likely there is competition from other websites for high search engine ranking results from the same keyword. For example, "San Francisco pediatric dentist" might result in far less competition than "dentist" or "pediatric dentist" or even "San Francisco dentist." Also useful in determining keywords is researching what keywords competitors use.

There are a number of free and premium tools available on the Web that can aid in researching and selecting keywords.

Don't expect the identification of your keywords and the submission of your pages to the search engines to result in an immediate flood of traffic to your site. First, many of the search engines take a number of weeks to process your submission. Second, some search engines rank based on a number of factors including site popularity.

If a local audience is important, consider having a page specifically optimized for the local area. It can be a mirror of your home page but contain and focus on keywords that attract the local demographic.

Related Questions

➡ 4. What is my brand's objective? **Page 13**

➡ 6. Who is my target audience? **Page 20**

➡ 15. How do I set up a website? **Page 60**

➡ 73. How do I track what is said about my brand? **Page 202**

Action Item

➡ Using **Alexa.com** or a similar website, check and see what keywords people are already using to find your site and see if you can build on that.

70. Should I Look at My Web Code?

Importance

Semantic code is a term used frequently by web developers in their sales pitches. To the average user, this may not mean much, but in the realm of web development, it means that the code used to create a site is written in a way that a computer can understand what it is supposed to be displaying to users with as few characters as possible.

The Internet operates off of *web standards*. These web standards are created by an international web consortium known as the W3C. These standards are created for both developers and end users. When browsers are made, such as Firefox, Safari, Chrome, and even Internet Explorer, they are developed in a way that enables them to "read" the code for a website and display it in a styled format to the end user. If web developers write website code in a manner that adheres to the web standards, it is easier for the browser to understand what it is supposed to display. The theory behind this practice is the cleaner the code, the easier it is for the search engines to read. Having clean, concise code enables a search engine to take less time to crawl the site and results in more favorable results.

There are times when displaying websites or code in its styled format isn't possible. Sometimes images don't load properly, there is a broken link to style settings, or a browser isn't enabling the images or styles to show. In this scenario, properly written semantic code helps to show alternative content. Coding all images and titles to have this alternative content to show in these scenarios works toward ensuring that search engines can properly read all the code, even in a situation when something breaks.

> Don't design your website without considering SEO. Make sure your web designer understands your expectations for organic SEO. Doing a retrofit on your shiny, new Flash-based site after it is built won't cut it. Spiders can crawl text, but they cannot crawl Flash or images. With images, make sure you use captions so that search engines can crawl those instead.

> Excess or complicated code can slow down a website. Combine files and clean up code where you can to speed things up. Website load speed is a factor used in calculating search rankings.

Related Questions

➧ 15. How do I set up a website? **Page 60**

➧ 22. What can I install on my website to encourage conversations? **Page 75**

➧ 26. What is Google Reader? **Page 88**

➧ 68. What is SEO? **Page 190**

Action Item

➜ Optimize the text in your RSS feed just like you should with your posts and web pages. Use descriptive, keyword-rich text in your title and description.

71. Does Link Building Help My Website?

Importance

An ideal situation for a website is to have many links leading back to it. Like word-of-mouth referrals to a company, the theory is that a large number of links back to a website indicates a high level of quality and relevance to a specific topic.

By building links back to a website, you're essentially building a foundation of referrals that search engines can find and view as reputation boosters. Similarly, if those backlinks are on what the search engines view as high-quality sites, they will be more valuable than links placed on low-quality sites.

One of the biggest complaints about the web in general, particularly in the social web, is that there appears to be a lot of *spam*. Facebook requests or tweets often have links associated with these generally unwanted blog comments. Often, these spam issues are meant to just annoy but can lead to viruses or questionable content on the Web. Other times, spam is a link-building campaign for a different brand when it hopes for growing its own search engine rankings by creating the backlinks.

Because of this fairly high level of "gaming" in the system, back links don't typically improve rankings as a tactic used on its own.

> The key to good link building is to do the exchange with similar niche sites. Having a link from a Smoothie King site if your site is about insurance won't be a good fit. People who are at a Smoothie King site are more than likely not looking to learn about insurance.

Rule of Thumb   Give link love, get link love. Don't be stingy with linking out. Doing so can encourage others to link to you. When link building, think quality, not quantity. One single, good, authoritative link can do a lot more for you than a dozen poor quality links, which can actually hurt you.

 **Related Questions**

→ 34. Should I "guest blog"? **Page 102**

→ 42. What should I tweet about? **Page 120**

→ 47. How do I best use my Facebook Page? **Page 135**

→ 72. How can I use social media to help my SEO? **Page 199**

Action Item

→ Find out how many sites are currently linked to your site. Using **Alexa.com**, a renowned web information website, you can enter your web address and easily learn how many sites are linked to your site. It also lists the exact addresses for each link so that you can see how each website ranks on the Web.

72. How Can I Use Social Media to Help My SEO?

Importance

The immediate benefit of social media is the Google- and Bing-confirmed influence on SEO. In Danny Sullivan's interview with Google and Bing for SearchEngineLand.com in December 2010, Sullivan writes that Google and Bing both use *social rank* as a factor to determine the rank of page importance. This means that how authoritative and relevant a brand is on a service such as Twitter can influence how authoritative and relevant that brand's website is to a search engine.

The data and its influence on the overall rank as shown in search results is not directly correlated, but the presence of even the slightest bit of influence shows that having a Twitter account that provides useful, informative content that others users consume may be the difference between being on the first page of search results and the second page. Considering the attention span of the general public is getting shorter (hello, 140-character limit), not being on the first page (or at least the first few pages) of your target keyword searches can be detrimental to business.

Website traffic is also noted as a key factor in search-engine ranking, which is a factor that can be directly affected by social media. As a brand develops its social presence and establishes itself as a thought leader or key resource, links direct traffic back to the brand and improve website statistics that affect search-engine ranking.

In a social media campaign, a strong call to action can convert potential consumers to actual customers. If that call to action is to have people visit your website, you need to make sure that your site is found by users easily and easy to browse through when they get there. Different SEO tactics can help ensure that both of these happen.

> Cater to influential bloggers and authority sites that might link to you and your images, videos, podcasts, and so on, or ask to reprint your content.

Rule of Thumb   Check out your social media profiles. Do they contain links back to your website? Many brands forget to include this on a Twitter or Facebook bio. Make sure that your website address is everywhere!

Related Questions

→ 68. What is SEO? **Page 190**

→ 70. Should I look at my web code? **Page 195**

→ 73. How do I track what is said about my brand? **Page 202**

→ 76. Do I still need a business card? **Page 214**

Action Item

→ Go to each of your social profiles and create a link to your website if you don't already have one.

Chapter 11

Monitoring an Online Brand

In this chapter:

- → **73. How do I track what is said about my brand?**
- → **74. What brand-monitoring tools can I use?**
- → **75. How can social media websites make this easier?**

Importance

73. How Do I Track What Is Said About My Brand?

A common argument in favor of social media for brands is that conversations happen about your brand, or your industry, whether or not you take part in it. Through the proper use of social media, those conversations can be guided and controlled to deliver your message rather than have to react to feedback in an attempt to regain control of the message.

As social media blends more into interactive public relations, brands can find themselves using more online methods to interact, converse, and communicate with their consumers to maintain a proactive position rather than reactive.

Monitoring a brand online is more than just seeing how many times and in what context your brand name is mentioned. Checking how often a brand is mentioned in blogs and Twitter isn't enough anymore. Although brand monitoring can be highly statistical, it's not just about quantity—it's about quality.

The details behind the brand mentions are just as important as the number. One hundred separate people can mention a brand in a day, but if the majority of those mentions are negative in nature, those mentions can have an overall negative effect on your influence.

The use of tools to monitor brand presence online can move past the mere counting of how often a brand is mentioned and move more into the context and sentiment of the brand through its overall presence.

Context addresses the quality of comments or articles mentioning the brand. If the brand is named 30 times, but the majority of the mentions are from simple lists, the quality can remain relatively low and have little impact on your brand presence. If the context is more detailed and relevant to your brand's positioning, it is more likely to have a direct effect.

Similar to context, sentiment measures the ratio of negative comments compared to positive comments. Although some may argue that any press is good press, many would also say that bad press is simply bad. Sentiment helps you to review if the overall feeling about your brand is negative or positive.

Related Questions

➡ 4. How do I develop my brand strategy? **Page 13**

➡ 10. How do I brand my online identity? **Page 34**

➡ 93. What metrics should I use to gauge my return on investment? **Page 250**

➡ 100. Where do I go from here? **Page 265**

Action Item

➡ Make a list of what metrics are important for you to review and understand to make it easier for you to determine what brand monitoring tools are best for you.

Importance

74. What Brand-Monitoring Tools Can I Use?

Both free and premium tools for brand monitoring fill the market. For most personal or small brands, the combined use of various free services is often enough to get a good picture of what is said about the brand online. There are premium services, however, with fairly low rates that can achieve the same results as the free tools but with more efficiency. The suggested tools for your business can depend on how much time you have to put into monitoring your brand and how much money you have available in your budget.

Free Tools

For small businesses or consultants, and even some larger businesses, there is not usually much in terms of financial resources available for social media monitoring tools. Because the whole concept of social media is still fairly new to most businesses, marketing budgets haven't had time to adjust to the costs associated with managing online brands. Free tools are available for brands that need to start analyzing data without placing a huge dent in their budgets.

Google Alerts

Google has a free tool called Google Alerts that you can use in many different ways. This service emails you when new web pages are published relevant to the keyword or phrase that you entered for the alert.

Go to /www.google.com/alerts. Here you can find a simple box to fill out to get alerts emailed to you, when it finds new results for keywords you enter. Start by putting in your company name, selecting Comprehensive, As-It-Happens, and your email address.

Then confirm your email address. Google then sends an email to the address you used for the alert. Click the link in the email to confirm you want the alert.

You can also create a Google Account to manage your alerts. I highly recommend doing this because it enables you to see all your different alerts and options on a single page. In short, it enables you to easily manage them.

Now that you know how to set up an alert, following are some tips for using Google Alerts like an expert:

- **Track your company**—If you plan to bring your brand online, taking the step to monitor anything being said about your brand online is an important one. Setting up your alerts or notifications to know when your site is mentioned online in a tweet, post, article, or news piece can help ensure you have a full picture of your online brand.

- **Track your products and industry**—You should track any terms that are unique to your company brand and then expand it to keywords in your industry. This enables you to know whether bloggers or news sites write about your products or company.

- **Track people within your company**—Set up alerts for the other people at your company, particularly those whose names and faces may be synonymous with your brand. If any blogs or news articles mention any of you, the alerts will let you know so that you can track not just your brand, but the people representing it as well.

- **Track the competition**—Don't just track yourself and your company. Keep an eye on what the competition does. As a real estate agent or hair salon, knowing what the competition is up to can help you keep your edge and stay ahead of the game.

HOOTSUITE

Hootsuite doubles as a tool to update statuses on a variety of networks, including Twitter, Facebook, LinkedIn, and Foursquare, while keeping track of your overall consumer statistics. The analytics area of Hootsuite tracks how many people take action on the tweets or updates you post. You can look at graphs that show how well your individual updates do, and whether people click links, retweet, or otherwise read what your brand has to say. What makes Hootsuite most useful is its capability to produce these statistics for the multiple sites, accounts, or profiles at one time, making your analytic research more efficient.

TWITTER COUNTER

If follower counts are important to you, Twitter Counter can prove to be a useful tool. It's graphical display of Twitter statistics that shows trends in counts for the number of people following your Twitter account and the number of people you follow. It also provides estimations for Twitter growth so that you can estimate how long it takes to reach a certain follower number if you continue your current trend. Twitter Counter's statistics focus solely on the quantity, not engagement or influence (see Figure 11-1).

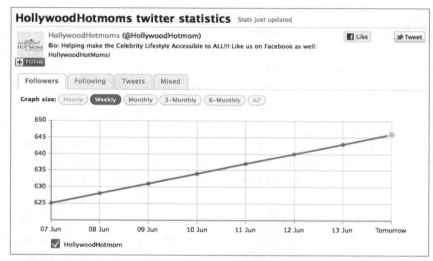

FIGURE 11-1: Twitter Counter ranks based on follower count.

SOCIAL MENTION

Social Mention, like Google Alerts, offers email updates for statistics. Social Mention spans the web tracking content containing keywords that you specify. You can target the alert to include specific types of content, including news, videos, blogs, bookmarks, events, audio, questions, comments, images, and microblogs. It also has a widget available for users to include these real-time statistics on their websites. Key measurements included in Social Mention's statistics include sentiment, reach, retweet, unique authors, and average time between mentions.

KLOUT

Klout, self-described as the "standard for influence," combines statistics from one Twitter account and one Facebook profile (with support for LinkedIn coming soon). According to Klout, overall online influence is based on the size of an engaged audience, how that audience is engaged, and who composes that audience (see Figure 11-2). Using these different metrics, Klout gives an overall score ranging from 1 to 100. The higher the score, the larger and stronger the influence of a brand is according to Klout. Even brands with smaller audience sizes can have high Klout scores if the audience is highly engaged.

FIGURE 11-2: Klout measures your online influence on Twitter, Facebook, and LinkedIn.

PEERINDEX

Using the term *authority*, PeerIndex measures a brand's ranking using eight key benchmarks including topic resonance (or relevance), audience, activity, and realness (the lack of spam activity).

BIT.LY

Most useful for tracking link consumption, Bit.ly provides a way to shorten long website addresses for use throughout the Web. As people click the link, Bit.ly tracks how many times the original link is posted on the Web and how many times those link clicks were attributed to your postings. URL shorteners are increasing in popularity because of the character limitations that so many services (such as Twitter) impose on their users.

CROWDBOOSTER

Crowdbooster provides insights on social media accounts down to an individual tweet level. The service details who retweets your information, how many times a tweet displays (impressions), and how broad your reach for each tweet was based on those other factors. Customized PDF and Excel reports can be generated, and reports can include information such as follower growth, reach, follower information, and "volume." It has a built-in recommendations engine, which provides performance statistics from the past and uses these statistics to help determine actionable items moving forward. Currently, the program is in private beta, and users must be approved before they can use the service. It is not yet known what the pricing structure will be after Crowdbooster leaves beta status.

Your first Google Alert should be set up to contain information about your brand name, with the selections being comprehensive, as-it-happens, and email.

Premium Tools

In the world of online monitoring tools, more and more paid services are popping up. They all claim to give the user the best information and perspective on what people say and feel about a brand. Following is a list of some of the more popular paid services available.

SOCIAL REPORT

With packages starting at only $9 per month, Social Report is priced for individuals, small businesses, marketers, and agencies. Jason Falls of Social Media Explorer is quoted as calling Social Report "Google Analytics for Social Media." The reports available include demographics, executive summaries of statistics, geographical reports, discovery agents for keyword research, and analyses of content based on goals and objectives. Social Report can also track sentiment and mentions of a brand. Reports are exportable into PDF and Excel formats.

COMPETE

Compete (see Figure 11-3) is similar to Google Analytics, with its statistics focused on websites such as traffic, keywords, audience profiles, referral sources, search, page views, and more. However, Compete can bring up information for other websites—not just your own. This could be a useful tool for brands needing to do competitor research to develop their own foundation. There is actually a Compare Site feature so that you can directly compare your own site to that of your competitors. Although Compete does have a free component, most of the features or statistics are only available to users under the Professional plan, which gives you the ability to see detailed SEO information about your site as well as the data of your competitors. Pricing starts at $199 for the Intro level of service.

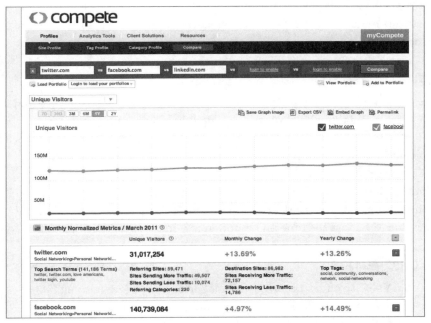

FIGURE 11-3: Compete enables you to compare sites to review statistics side by side.

RADIAN6

Radian6, recently acquired by Salesforce, is a service that states its product can scan more than 100,000 million websites for mentions about brands. The sites scanned include mainstream news, blogs, videos, and social media. All the data is found in real time. Thus you can find who talks about your brand and find the most influential people as it happens. Radian6 offers comprehensive analytics and enables deep filtering, social media metrics, and creating data breakdown.

HUBSPOT

Hubspot is a robust service that bills itself as "an all-in-one marketing software platform for small and medium-sized businesses." Its software helps brands to create, optimize, and publicize content and then analyze content effectiveness to evaluate brand return on investment (ROI). Hubspot tracks full marketing efforts, including leads, social networks, email campaigns, blogs, and websites. In addition to these premium services, Hubspot has free tools available to brands that "grade" various marketing efforts including alerts, websites, press releases, social network accounts, and even books.

SM2

SM2 is software created for PR and marketing agencies to monitor and measure social media. This product enables you to follow conversations and review the positive and the negative sentiment people feel for brands, clients, and competitors across many social media channels. These channels include blogs, wikis, social networks, video sites, and photo-sharing sites. Its reporting types include comparison charts and themed reports that make it easy to identify daily volume, demographics, location, and the tone and emotion of what is said.

TOPIC VELOCITY

Topic Velocity offers a monitoring tool priced per user, per topic. It provides users with information on the rate of change of sentiment about a particular topic. The tool also produces data on conversation topics, tone and sentiment ratings, topic trending, competitive monit oring, topic and issue discovery, source identification, topic tagging, workflow and engagement, and alerting tools.

TRACKUR

Trackur is a flexible monitoring tool similar to Radian 6. Trackur looks at web pages, including blogs, images, and forums. It then notifies a user of keyword findings or related interest items. Trackur enables comprehensive social media monitoring. It then alerts its users by sending custom alerts, tracking sentiment and trends.

This is just a short list of the many paid services available today. More and more types of these services pop up all the time.

Many premium services offer a free trial option. Take advantage of the free trials so that you can get a glimpse of how the premium services can help you to grow your brand and see if you can continue the same type of analytical research after the trial is over.

Related Questions

➡ 13. How do I choose which sites to use? **Page 52**

➡ 77. Why does what I do in the real world matter? **Page 216**

➡ 87. How do I get support from social media websites? **Page 242**

➡ 97. How can I build influence? **Page 258**

Action Item

➡ Set up your social profiles on any of the listed free tools and get a feel for what kind of information you can extract from brand monitoring services. You can then build on this foundation and create your own monitoring dashboard or move on to a premium service when you have a better idea of what information you want to track.

Importance

75. How Can Social Media Websites Make This Easier?

Analytical tools are quickly adding information obtained from services such as Twitter and Facebook because the social conversation makes it easy for statistics on sentiment to be read. In traditional marketing, research was often cumbersome and costly because brands had to reach out to customers to understand their sentiments. With the advent of social media, the conversations about brands are no longer just taking place at the water cooler; conversations are taking place online, and these analytical tools can capture those sentiments as they happen.

As brands take better advantage of this new ability to capture information on a virtually real-time basis, research takes less time to complete, and more time to address issues is available.

An added benefit of social media analytics websites is the capability to combine both website information and social statistics to provide an overall review of digital marketing efforts.

 Related Questions

➧ 2. Brand, online presence—What's the difference? **Page 4**

➧ 12. What social networks best fit my goals? **Page 40**

➧ 52. How do Facebook "likes" help me? **Page 150**

➧ 72. How can I use social media to help my SEO? **Page 199**

Action Item

➧ Looking at your alerts and brand-monitoring tool data, compare how much of the online information about your brand is from a social site or blog and how much is from a "traditional" news website.

Chapter 12

The Real World

In this chapter:

- 76. Do I still need a business card?
- 77. Why does what I do in the real world matter?
- 78. How do I find (and get) speaking engagements?
- 79. What is a Tweet-up?
- 80. How do I use event-planning websites?
- 81. What are tips for hosting a successful event?

Importance

76. Do I Still Need a Business Card?

The short answer to the question, "Do I still need a business card?" is a resounding "yes!"

There are a number of mobile and web applications that seek to replace the traditional business card. Some of these services want to enable the trading of information through quick response (QR) code, bumping phones, Twitter hashtags, email exchanges, or friending.

Although all these services certainly make trading information easy and efficient, the bottom line is that not everybody uses them. If your core audience is another business or brand that is heavy into social media and tech, these services may be sufficient for your needs. However, business trends come and go, and no normal standard exists for exchanging business information other than the business card (see Figure 12-1).

> **?**
> A QR code is a 2-D barcode that can be scanned by a smart phone, and then downloads information embedded in the QR code into the phone.

FIGURE 12-1: My business card has both traditional and social information on it.

Many professionals in the tech and social media bubble automatically assume that everyone has an email address, website, Twitter handle, Facebook page, and LinkedIn profile. For the average person, however, even a branded email address (such as dave@bullfrog-media.com) is hard to come by let alone a website or social media profile.

A business card should always be kept handy. If someone you meet doesn't want to use technology to trade information, you at least have the business card to fall back on. On your business card should be all the information pertinent to keeping in contact.

 Related Questions

➜ 1. Why do I need a personal brand? **Page 2**

➜ 10. How do I brand my online identity? **Page 34**

➜ 11. Why does an email address matter? **Page 36**

➜ 77. Why does what I do in the real world matter? **Page 216**

Action Item

➜ Take a look at your business card. Does it contain what your audience considers the important information? If you find yourself always writing additional information on your card, such as your cell phone number, consider redesigning your card so that you have it already included.

Importance

77. Why Does What I Do in the Real World Matter?

A brand should always be represented online as it is offline. What the web does is open up the audience to a broader level. A person in Australia can buy a skateboard from a shop in California. Friends across the world from each other can hop onto a computer and visit with each other face to face via services such as Skype. Companies can close multibillion dollar deals with the exchange of an email.

When an online brand develops a reputation online, people expect to see that reputation carried out in real life. Conversely, an offline presence should be properly represented online. Social media should be viewed as another tool to carry out the overall marketing objectives of a brand and not as a primary avenue for business development. Because of this, it's essential to remember that offline activities, including both business and personal activities, reflect the brand and how current and potential consumers perceive it.

During a social media campaign, brands should make sure that all actions have the campaign's best interest as the main focus. If the campaign is to position the brand as a leader in geo-location, the brand and its team should focus on events circling this particular world. Actions, both offline and online, need to support each other and be unified in its efforts to reach a goal for that effort to be successful.

During SXSW Interactive 2011, I happened to share a cab ride with another person who I didn't know. To make conversation, I asked him what brought him to Austin. He then told me that he was there to just "check things out" because he and his partner were starting a business in San Francisco. I found this interesting because I am from the San Francisco area, and wanted to know more about what his business was about. I asked him, and he didn't want to share. He gave me little tidbits, letting me know that it involved helping elementary schools with fundraising, but only very general details. Of course, many companies like to be quiet about their activities to prevent any intellectual property theft issues, so I did understand if he had privacy concerns. Instead of pushing things further, I let him know that my company was heavily involved with education and fundraising, and that my partner was on the executive board for several education-related foundations or organizations, and that when he was ready I would love the opportunity to talk more about it. I asked him if he had a business card, and he said that he forgot to order cards before he went to Austin. So, instead, I handed him mine and mentioned that he could also get a hold of me on LinkedIn or Twitter. He then told me that he didn't use either, and didn't really understand the point of the services.

By this point, I lost any interest in future contact. I hadn't yet even had an opportunity to visit his website, but because of the pure lack of interest in holding or ability to have a conversation about what his business was about (at a networking conference, mind you), it didn't matter if his business had the best online presence in the world. The offline presence was so poor that the first impression I had of his company was negative already. The most difficult thing to digest about this conversation was the fact that I had already expressed an interest in either using his product or becoming involved in some other way if he had that desire.

Don't rely too heavily on one way of marketing your brand. If you're going to be super duper active and making connections in person, make sure your website or online presence will be able to address questions that people have when they visit it for more information. If your brand is going to be very developed online, make sure that the people marketing it in person are able to describe what you do and accurately represent your brand.

 Related Questions

- → 1. Why do I need a personal brand? **Page 2**
- → 7. Am I reflecting my brand? **Page 22**
- → 10. How do I brand my online identity? **Page 34**
- → 82. How do I handle inappropriate comments? **Page 228**

Action Item

- → Review your marketing plan. You should have stated objectives and goals in the plan for both offline and online efforts so that you make sure that what you do in real life properly reflects your brand.

Importance

78. How Do I Find (and Get) Speaking Engagements?

An "elevator pitch" is a short (typically about 20–30 second) brief about you for you to tell others more about you and your business in the time that it would take for you to ride in an elevator. After your brand has developed into a thought leader, invitations to speak at events can come in droves. Unfortunately, those speaking engagement invitations are not going to happen until you have developed yourself as both a thought leader and an established public speaker. To make that happen, you need to be proactive about finding speaking engagements and earning the invitations.

The key to speaking in front of people and being successful is to position yourself as the person in the room whom everyone wants to listen to. Even if you are a PR person speaking to a room of PR people, you need a quality that makes you stick out from everyone else. When you're at an event, always strive to put yourself in the position where even if you're not in the front of the room, other attendees should think that you belong there. Not being at the center of the room shouldn't stop you from talking to the other attendees (particularly during breaks or lunches), networking, and getting to know other people while letting them get to know you. Take advantage of the time that you have with other people and make sure that your elevator pitch is fine-tuned to the point where you can let people know more about your skill sets in an effective and efficient manner.

Local organizations such as Rotary clubs, chambers of commerce, and government organizations have events on a regular basis. Some of them want to start new series of events. Approach these organizations about the possibility of speaking or hosting an event. These smaller, more local audiences can help you to develop and fine-tune your message while you prepare for the bigger events.

As you grow your portfolio, start looking at events at which you want to speak. Most large events require that speakers submit presentation ideas for review. Because you have already had some experience talking in front of people, you should have a better idea of what people want to hear about and what your audience wants to hear from you.

Network with people involved with these events. Local organizations and large events alike are growing increasingly accessible through the social web. Starting a conversation online with these organizations can help provide an easy foundation to continue offline and make these speaking engagements that much easier to land.

As you speak at all these events, make sure that you're publicizing your involvement. People don't want to hear from people who have never spoken before. Publish your presentations on your website or on a social service such as Slideshare.com (see Figure 12-2). Have a speaker page on your website so that you can have a list of places where you've spoken that others can easily reference. Your resume or LinkedIn profile should also include your speaking engagements as part of your achievements.

Past Speaking Engagements

- BlogWorld New York 2011
- Town & Country Merchant Meeting
- SXSW 2011: My Kindergartner Markets Better than You
- United Nations Association Film Festival
- Social Media Strategies Summit
- Credit Union Bay Area Executive Coalition Conference
- BlogWorld & New Media Expo
- West Coast Songwriters Conference
- NetRoots Nation
- Community 2.0
- BlogWorld 2009
- SXSW 2010 Community Innovation Summit
- SXSW 2010: How To Score A Job
- SXSW 2009
- Social Media Summit 2010
- Social Media Strategies
- 140 Twitter Conference
- Virtual Worlds
- Silicon Valley Marketing Association
- International Association of Administrative Professionals
- Marketing in the Oilfield Conference
- NeoCon East

FIGURE 12-2: A speaking engagement page on your website helps archive past engagements like a resume.

Related Questions

➔ 4. How do I develop my brand strategy? **Page 13**

➔ 10. How do I brand my online identity? **Page 34**

➔ 93. What metrics should I use to gauge my return on investment? **Page 250**

➔ 100. Where do I go from here? **Page 265**

Action Item

➔ Write down your elevator pitch. Practice saying it to yourself until you feel comfortable with how you're presenting your business.

Importance

79. What Is a Tweet-Up?

When Twitter took off, one of the biggest trends was to take any word and add a "Tw" to the beginning of it. Considered by many to be both cute and annoying, this "Tw" trend made it easy for Twitter users to identify events or ideas as Twitter-specific.

A few words that have been Twitter-fied include:

➡ Tweet-up (meet-up)

➡ Twestival (Festival; this is also the name of a Twitter-specific festival established by @amanda)

➡ Twitterati (Glitterati)

➡ Twitterverse (Universe)

➡ Tweeps/Tweeple (Peeps/People)

➡ Twit-tastic (Fantastic)

Essentially, a Tweet-up is when people on Twitter meet up in real life. Tweet-ups are a way for people to take what they've established online and use it to network offline.

Some Tweet-ups take it a step further and even have "sponsors" who help provide entertainment by showcasing their products or services at the event. Like mini-exposition halls, it can be beneficial for these companies because the Tweet-ups are usually composed of specific target demographics.

Tweet-ups do not have to be technologically focused. Many people on Twitter are not involved directly with technology, even though they are using it to communicate. Tweet-ups can be about school, music, government, art, books, and virtually any other topic.

Locations for Tweet-ups can vary as well. Depending on your anticipated attendance, they can easily take place at a private residence, coffee shop, bar, restaurant, hotel, or convention center.

The most beneficial part of a Tweet-up is that it gives you an opportunity to discuss your product or service with a specific group of people in more than just 140 characters. Just like speaking engagements, Tweet-ups are a way for a brand to establish itself offline as a thought leader as conversations take place in real life with real-time feedback.

This is more proof that what you do in real life still matters. There needs to be personality behind an online presence for it to make a real impact on a brand, social media campaign, and so on.

 Related Questions

- ➔ 76. Do I still need a business card? **Page 214**
- ➔ 77. Why does what I do in the real world matter? **Page 216**
- ➔ 98. How can I keep my social media efforts interesting? **Page 261**
- ➔ 100. Where do I go from here? **Page 265**

Action Item

- ➔ Tweet-ups are a great way to actually meet the people you talk to online. If you want to build a better network, consider hosting or attending a Tweet-up to help make that happen.

Importance

80. How Do I Use Event-Planning Websites?

Event websites help both organizers and attendees make their networking plans. Depending on your need, these websites can do everything from help pick a date for an event to gathering RSVPs to selling tickets.

Consider the size of your event. Is this for a small group of people that you already know? Are you trying to establish a large event for international attendees? Take a look at the needs of your event first, and then check out the online options that can help make this a more efficient process.

If you need help determining a date and time for your event, services such as Doodle.com and Tungle.me enable attendees to rate options that work for them so that you can easily see what works for the group majority. Doodle.com also enables the options to be text-based so that you can collect information on more than just dates and times and look for input on things such as locations.

Services such as Plancast.com (see Figure 12-3) help you to review upcoming events. When you tell Plancast to "count you in" for an event, it lists your social avatar in the list of planned attendees. This social way of RSVPing helps you to visualize who else you know, or may want to know, will be at this event.

A slew of websites can help with ticketing. Eventbrite and Mogotix are two popular options for selling tickets or registration online and both come with nominal fees. Guest lists can be exported so that you can print with ease. Registrants receive tickets that also contain QR codes, so the codes can be scanned at the event for efficient check in.

Meetup.com is rapidly becoming a go-to website for event planning. Because you can use it for personal groups and large events, Meetup.com helps organizers to categorize and publicize events in virtually any manner that works for them. From organizing an at-home movie night among friends to creating a conference for thousands, Meetup.com provides an easy portal for both organizers and attendees.

If your event requires participation from others, such as volunteering shifts or potluck contributions, services such as Jooners utilize online sign-up sheets. These are particularly useful when real-time information needs to be shared among a number of users. Attendees don't need to have accounts with the service, and information can be changed later by using email addresses to "log on" and input new data.

FIGURE 12-3: Plancast enables you to see when your friends make plans to go to an event.

Related Questions

➡ 76. How do I develop my brand strategy? **Page 214**

➡ 81. What are tips to hosting a successful event? **Page 224**

➡ 87. How do I get support from social media websites? **Page 242**

➡ 98. How can I keep my social media efforts interesting? **Page 261**

Action Item

➡ Sign up for a free account with Plancast and start looking at different events already being publicized. Check out how they are integrating other event-planning sites like **Meetup.com**, Eventbrite, Facebook Events, or Mogotix and see which methods you like best.

Importance

81. What Are Tips for Hosting a Successful Event?

As a brand, your purpose in hosting an event should be clearly identified internally. As with any other marketing effort, these purposes and goals must be used as a foundation to build your metrics on, to later determine ROI.

Incorporating your event into your overall social media campaign means that your event should be social to be successful. Following are a few tips that can help:

➤ Publicize your event with your social profiles. What's the purpose of having a social event if your networks don't know you're having it? The event should be posted on all your social accounts, your website, and possibly even your email signature.

➤ Consider the use of a hashtag when you have your event. That way, when people are there and start talking about it on Twitter, you (and everyone else) can track the conversation by searching the hashtag.

➤ Use geolocation for people to "check in" to the event. Offering specials through geo-location applications such as Foursquare can also help broaden the reach of your event to people who come near the location in the days leading up to it. When people check in to your location, Foursquare allows them to see Specials Nearby. People who may not have otherwise heard about your event can now learn about it just by virtue of being nearby.

➤ If possible, stream your event using a service such as Ustream .tv. People who can't attend can take part in the action through these streaming services. Although it won't necessarily help you increase any profits, it can help build visibility and event recognition for the next time you have an event.

➤ Keep a photo album of your events as proof of its success to potential attendees for the next event. Facebook and other social sites have the capability to create online photo albums that can be referenced at a later time. Photos are also a great way to have an excuse to tag other people featured in the photos so that they share them with their network. Buzz about your event after the fact can help to get more people interested in attending the next one.

Google Alerts can help you create an archive for your hashtags. Twitter search is fairly robust and inclusive but does not archive hashtag usage forever.

Related Questions

- 5. What is my brand's objective? **Page 18**
- 77. Why does what I do in the real world matter? **Page 216**
- 79. What is a "Tweet-up?" **Page 220**
- 93. What do I include as my next steps? **Page 250**

Action Item

- Collect photos that you may have taken from past events and set them up as albums on your Facebook page. If you haven't had an event yet, but plan to, post pictures of things related to event coordination, such as boxes of fliers being delivered or images of other companies that may somehow be involved in the event.

Chapter 13

Dealing with Difficult Situations

In this chapter:

Importance

82. How Do I Handle Inappropriate Comments?

Inappropriate comments can come in a variety of forms. The most common inappropriate comment is spam but can also be comments that use vulgar content, are unrelated to the topic at hand, or directly offend others.

The general unspoken rule is that inappropriate comments should be left alone. The social web is supposed to be one that enables open, two-way communication between parties regardless of whether the varying parties agree on a topic. Part of keeping a social web conversation "real" is allowing people to express differing opinions.

When inappropriate comments are posted, the usual reaction is a desire to delete the comment in question. Brands should resist this temptation, however, because it can actually be viewed more negatively against the brand as censorship. Instead, consider some alternative options.

Ignore It

Addressing inappropriate comments head-on can often "add fuel to the fire." If someone is upset or angry or just plain out of line, responding to the comments can make things worse. Engaging the offenders in a conversation surrounding their comment essentially gives their negativity life and the brand's action becomes reactive.

Don't be tempted to respond to inappropriate comments if you feel as if the response might result in an argument or put you on the defensive. You should never feel like you have to defend your brand. Instead, if you do respond, the response should be something that supports your stance instead of something that positions the other side in a negative slant.

Also, don't forget that there is a big difference between criticisms and inappropriate comments. Inappropriate comments are comments that have nothing to do with the topic, use excessive (or any) vulgarity or profanity, or use other statements that are intended to offend. Criticisms, on the other hand, are points of view that might differ from your own. People are entitled to have their own opinions, even if they don't match yours. Differing opinions or criticisms aren't necessarily inappropriate and actually give you an opportunity to have other perspectives addressed.

Address It

Sometimes a comment needs to be addressed, and there isn't any other way around it. This is not a bad thing. Part of the beauty of the social web is having this newfound ability to communicate directly with people. When your brand is put in the position of responding to inappropriate or negative comments, it is your brand's opportunity to show how well you can handle a bad situation.

Local San Carlos wine bar @flightloungeCA wrote a tweet on its account that said that it had received enormous amounts of pressure from "PROs" that would affect live music events at the bar. The city's assistant city manager retweeted the @flightloungeCA tweet to our @bullfrogmedia account and asked us who was pressuring the wine bar. The reason that the assistant city manager asked us directly was that we had just finished tweeting a compliment to @flightloungeCA, calling it one of the city's "secret, underappreciated treasures." We responded that we didn't know what "PROs" were, but that perhaps it was local eateries that also featured professional live music on the same night.

We were informed by @flightloungeCA that "PRO" stands for Professional Rights Organization, which has to do with musician and artist copyrights. Then, @flightloungeCA made the comment to @bullfrogmedia that we had mentioned eateries that were not truly "locally owned and operated." We responded that we thought that was incorrect, as one of the locations they were refuting "local status" for was The Office Bar & Grill and the others mentioned were all supporters of the local community. In turn, @flightloungeCA proceeded to continue the discussion by defending its location as a bigger supporter than the others.

Rather than go on the defensive, it might have been better for @flightloungeCA to either not say anything or comment about how it supported the community and it encouraged others to do the same. What would have been even better would have been if @flightloungeCA recognized that both an influencer in city politics and an obvious fan took interest in the future of the business. It could have reached two more people to gain more community support.

In truth, however, we could have also avoided arguing about the statement we believed was incorrect. It obviously started an argument that neither could win (see Figure 13-1).

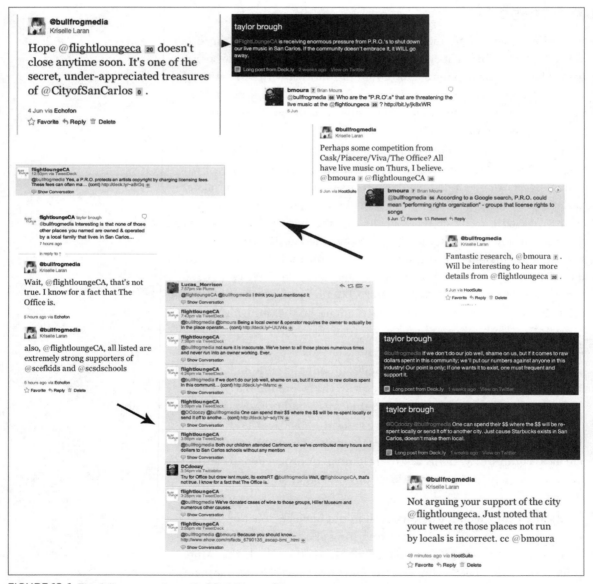

FIGURE 13-1: The full conversation with @flightloungeCA

Delete It

If you have no other choice, you can always delete inappropriate material. This option should be used selectively. Take a look at your brand and the inappropriate comment. How "inappropriate" is it? Is your product or service focused on children? Is an inappropriate comment composed of vulgar language? If the answer is yes, delete the comment.

If the inappropriate comment attacks you or team members in a slanderous fashion, there can be a strong argument made for deleting the comment. But before you do, look at it to see if you can respond in a way that doesn't give credit to the author but instead shows your audience that the comment has no grounds.

Essentially, before you take action against inappropriate content, make sure you're truly doing it because it is inappropriate and not just because you don't agree with what is said.

> When in doubt, don't delete. Try to ignore inappropriate comments if possible, and don't engage people who try to provoke negative reactions.

Related Questions

➤ 4. How do I develop my brand strategy? **Page 13**

➤ 7. Am I reflecting my brand? **Page 22**

➤ 14. Why do I need to be selective? **Page 56**

➤ 73. How do I track what is said about my brand? **Page 202**

Action Item

➤ Consider creating a place on your website, blog, or social media profiles where you address actions that you will take against vulgar or offensive language.

Importance

83. What if I'm Stalked?

Social networks have security settings that can help prevent these issues. When online, the best way to approach security is to remember that anything you post online can be accessed by anyone regardless of whether you make it "private." That said, as a brand that wants to establish its online presence, staying quiet isn't going to do anything to help your social media campaign.

Your social media campaign strategy should have an ultimate goal to build your brand. If your brand is built around a specific individual, chances of being stalked through social profiles do increase. However, this can be limited by taking the necessary precautions by not sharing more than what is necessary.

The easiest way to invite stalking is to use geolocation tools to place you at specific locations that do nothing to further your brand presence. If you tend to frequent locations that don't promote the brand, don't check in. Your frequency at these locations establishes a pattern in your habits that potential stalkers can study and use to their advantage later on. For example, if you check in at places such as "Home," with your address listed on the application map, you're basically inviting other people to come visit. Even without listing the specific address, the coordinates of the location you create are placed on a map in the general area, and it's easy for a potential stalker to come to the area and wait to see where you live.

Be careful who you connect with online. Don't forget—the quantity of followers is not as important as the quality of followers. Before clicking "Accept" on your Foursquare app, take a look at the profile of the person who wants to connect. If you're not in the habit of checking into private locations, you can be a little bit more lax with this point than other people.

If you don't want anyone to know where you are, there is a simple solution: Don't check in! Although there is an Off the Grid option in services such as Foursquare that enable you to check in without telling others, what's the point?

As a brand, consider using the Tips or Recommendations features of geolocation applications instead of the Check In feature. This can help establish your position as an expert in the local area rather than as a frequent consumer.

For Twitter and Facebook, the same rules apply. Don't post what you don't want people to know. Unfortunately, even with the most stringent security measures in place, the action of placing your information on a social network makes the information just that—social. If you have private information that you don't want to open up to potential stalkers, simply don't post it. That includes birth dates, family members' names, phone numbers, and most important, addresses.

Use common sense. If you don't want something to be viewed or known by others, don't post it.

Related Questions

➜ 4. How do I develop my brand strategy? **Page 13**

➜ 5. What is my brand's objective? **Page 18**

➜ 7. Am I reflecting my brand? **Page 22**

➜ 10. How do I brand my online identity? **Page 34**

Action Item

➜ If you use a geo-location application already, look at your check-in history. If you've been checking into fast food restaurants and you're presenting yourself online as a health fanatic, you may want to reconsider your use of the application.

Importance

84. How Do I Prevent Spam?

Spam is an ever-growing problem on the social web. Most social sites provide an option to report spam, but it's getting harder to prevent from happening in the first place. Before connecting with people on services such as Twitter, look at their profiles first. Their content is a good indicator of whether they spam, and good content can help prevent your account from attracting spam.

For your own website, other measures can prevent spam from invading your email or blog. These include:

➜ Don't list your email address. When spam bots scan the web looking for email addresses, they look at the format of the text. If they see dave@bullfrog-media.com, they see that it's an email address and they can collect it for later use. However, if they see something like dave [at] bullfrog-media.com, it won't be recognized by a bot even if it still is actually linked to my address through the use of HTML code.

➜ Use CAPTCHAs for forms. With a little bit of coding, you can require people to answer a question or decipher an image before they can submit comments to a blog or respond to a contact form.

➜ Use a form for people to contact you through your website rather than giving out your email address. This can help you to keep your email address more private, for you to distribute as you choose rather than for people to collect it.

➜ Moderate content. With services such as Disqus or the built-in Wordpress or Blogger moderation features, you can require comments to be approved before they get posted on your site. You can also require users to log in before commenting (see Figure 13-2). Additional settings for moderation include requiring commenters to have a previous comment approved before a subsequent comment gets posted. Apply "nofollow" to the links on your blog. Take away the ability for websites to receive credit for back links from your site. Wordpress and Blogger are already set up to use nofollow, but make sure that any plug-ins you install don't interfere with the "nofollow" feature. If your blog does follow, spam bots may be more attracted to your website because of the reciprocal search engine "credit" that it receives from having a back link.

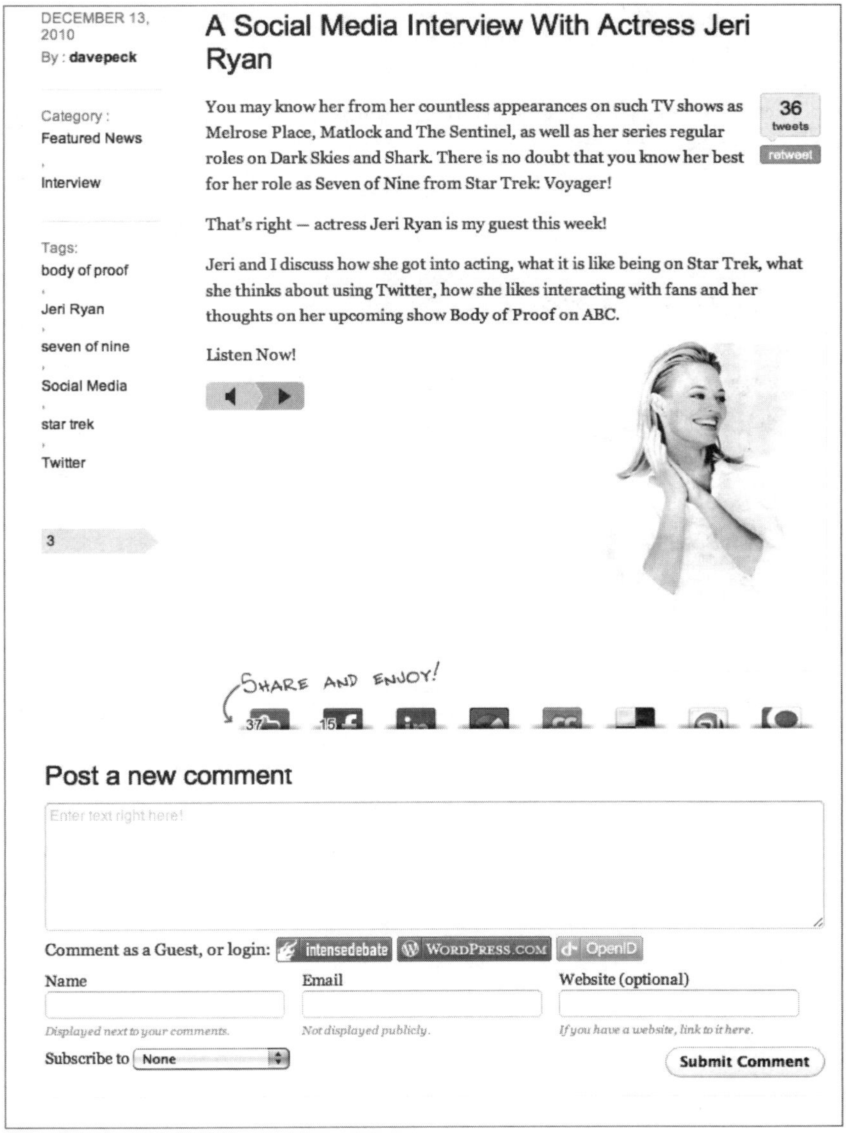

DECEMBER 13, 2010
By : **davepeck**

Category :
Featured News

,

Interview

Tags:
body of proof

,

Jeri Ryan

,

seven of nine

,

Social Media

,

star trek

,

Twitter

3

A Social Media Interview With Actress Jeri Ryan

You may know her from her countless appearances on such TV shows as Melrose Place, Matlock and The Sentinel, as well as her series regular roles on Dark Skies and Shark. There is no doubt that you know her best for her role as Seven of Nine from Star Trek: Voyager!

That's right — actress Jeri Ryan is my guest this week!

Jeri and I discuss how she got into acting, what it is like being on Star Trek, what she thinks about using Twitter, how she likes interacting with fans and her thoughts on her upcoming show Body of Proof on ABC.

Listen Now!

36 tweets

retweet

SHARE AND ENJOY!

37   15

Post a new comment

Enter text right here!

Comment as a Guest, or login: intensedebate | WORDPRESS.COM | OpenID

Name
Displayed next to your comments.

Email
Not displayed publicly.

Website (optional)
If you have a website, link to it here.

Subscribe to [None ▾]

Submit Comment

FIGURE 13-2: Requiring users to log in before commenting can help prevent spam.

Related Questions

➔ 7. Am I reflecting my brand? **Page 22**

➔ 22. What can I install on my website to encourage conversations? **Page 75**

➔ 32. What is a CAPTCHA? **Page 98**

➔ 37. Are there any tips or tricks to interacting on other websites? **Page 109**

Action Item

➔ If you have a WordPress blog, activate the built-in Akismet plugin. This plugin helps to filter spam.

85. Can I Stop People from Hacking?

Importance

The two networks that have had the biggest issues with hacking are Twitter and Facebook. The most prevalent way to hack into other accounts is through the use of bad links that convince people to enter their username and password. Thinking that they are just logging back into a service, this information is actually collected by a *phishing* link that has nothing to do with the network services. Then, as spammers or hackers collect these usernames and passwords, viruses or other bad content can spread through the social account.

Everyone is always on the alert when it comes to Facebook. Each week, news breaks that yet another FB hacking or phishing attempt is making its rounds through the popular social network.

In Facebook's enhanced privacy and security settings, there is now a way to help ensure your account is protected against these harmful attempts to attack your account.

1. In the drop-down menu located at the top-right side of your Facebook account, go to Account Settings.

2. Next to the Account Security subheading, click Change.

3. Select Secure Browsing (https). Set up your account to use secure browsing sessions every time you log into Facebook by enabling the Browse Facebook on a Secure Connection (https) Whenever Possible box (see Figure 13-3).

The "s" in "https" indicates that your session is secured. Websites that require security, such as banks, encrypt the sessions of their users to help ensure protection and maintain the integrity of the data.

Account Security
Set up secure browsing (https) and login alerts.

Secure Browsing (https)
☑ Browse Facebook on a secure connection (https) whenever possible

When a new computer or mobile device logs into this account:
☐ Send me an email

Save

Computers and mobile devices currently associated with your account:
Device Name   Time Saved

FIGURE 13-3: Select Secure Browsing to help limit spam and hacking issues with your Facebook experience.

On Twitter, make sure that you keep your password secure. When other websites ask you to connect to theirs through Twitter, you should never have to give them your Twitter password. Instead, you'll be redirected to Twitter to give that particular website authorization to log you in through the Twitter system.

To see which sites or applications you've authorized to access your Twitter account for login, posting, or other statistical purposes, you can check your Twitter settings, and go to Applications for the full list (see Figure 13-4).

FIGURE 13-4: Check your settings on Twitter to see whom you have authorized.

To prevent hacking on your website, make sure you keep your access settings secure and updated. WordPress, in particular, updates its framework frequently to consistently patch or improve the security of their coding. Keep up to date with improvements and upgrade whenever possible (see Figure 13-5).

WordPress 3.1.3 is available! Please update now.

FIGURE 13-5: Update your WordPress blog when you get the notification.

Don't click links from people you don't know. If you do know the person, but question the content or the link, just don't click it. You can easily Google or research the content to see if it's a phishing attempt if you actually want to know.

Related Questions

➜ 15. How do I set up a website? **Page 60**

➜ 32. What is a CAPTCHA? **Page 98**

➜ 68. What is SEO? **Page 190**

➜ 70. Should I look at my web code? **Page 195**

Action Item

➜ Check your Facebook, Twitter, and blog settings and update your passwords or revoke application access as necessary.

86. What Can I Do if Someone Is Upset by Other Comments?

Similar to inappropriate behavior, if someone is upset by another person's comments, further action can be determined by the overall objectives of the social media strategy and campaign.

The level of concern displayed by the offended party doesn't actually matter. The fact that they are upset to begin with means that you should take every measure necessary to address the concern and provide them with the utmost in service needed for the issues to be dealt with head on.

Rule of Thumb   Be proactive, not reactive. If a response doesn't help, don't do it.

The action toward the offender, however, does vary depending on how the action reflects on your brand. If responding directly to the offender causes a negative reaction, handling the situation by addressing the upset party might be the best way to deal.

A situation where one person upsets another is a test for your brand. You can be either reactive or proactive. Often, the proactive road is the one that deals with rectifying the situation with the offended party.

Just like with inappropriate comments, though, there is only so much attention that should be paid to either situation. Brands have to take care to not cross the line that causes a negative issue to become worse. Refer to our conversation from Figure 13-1 if you need a refresher on how things can continue to go downhill if too much attention is given to something that is already negative.

 Related Questions

➜   4. How do I develop my brand strategy? **Page 13**

➜   10. How do I brand my online identity? **Page 34**

➜   93. What metrics should I use to gauge my return on investment? **Page 250**

➜   100. Where do I go from here? **Page 265**

Action Item

➜ Be proactive and review comments. If comments get out of hand, know how to shut down a thread. Practice.

Importance

87. How Do I Get Support from Social Media Websites?

Most social media websites have a support feature available to its users. You might need support for various reasons, but know that there are limits to the support available.

Help centers from places such as Twitter and Facebook address specific things: the basics for getting started on the services, areas to report violations, advertising, and server status. The guides are fairly inclusive, with how-to information on almost every part of being a part of the services. What you won't find online is information on strategy or campaigns. These websites offer a service that they expect users to run in a way they see fit. Although there are often rules and etiquette, most of the guidelines (if the site doesn't address them specifically in any guides or terms of service) are actually established by the users rather than the site itself.

The links to support areas of the websites can often be found in the footer or on the side of the site. Typically, the link names are Help, Support, Status, or Feedback.

> Support sites should answer most of your questions. If they don't, and how-to guides can't answer your questions, consider contacting a social media specialist.

 Related Questions

- → 2. Brand, online presence—What's the difference? **Page 4**
- → 5. What is my brand's objective? **Page 18**
- → 75. How can social media websites make this easier? **Page 212**
- → 100. Where do I go from here? **Page 265**

Action Item

- → Make sure you know where the support pages on your social networks are, and when contacting them, make sure you give them as much info as possible so that they know how to help you.

Creating a Social Media Strategy

Importance

88. What Does a Social Media Strategy Look Like?

A documented social media strategy should always be developed prior to beginning any social media campaign. Particularly in situations where multiple people will represent a brand online, a documented strategy will help to ensure that everyone is on the same page and understands the brand's overall goals and objectives for developing and growing its online presence. Having it written ensures that everyone involved received the same information and reduces risk of misunderstandings or misinterpretations.

Social media strategies can vary in style, detail, and size, but you do want to make sure that it includes the essentials: a definition of what your intention for being online is and what you view as success in your efforts.

A high-level strategy is often sufficient for small to medium-sized businesses. "High-level" means that the information contained within the document highlights the overall objectives and plan for execution of presence development, but does not itemize individual tasks and responsibilities.

Larger businesses, or brands intending to invest a significant amount of resources and finances in a social media campaign, should have a much more detailed strategy written that covers each itemized objective and plan for implementation.

"Significant" does not have to equal millions of dollars. If the resources you spend on social media are a large portion of your individual budget, then it can be considered significant.

Related Questions

➤ 4. How do I develop my brand strategy? **Page 13**

➤ 10. How do I brand my online identity? **Page 34**

➤ 93. What metrics should I use to gauge my return on investment? **Page 250**

➤ 100. Where do I go from here? **Page 265**

Action Item

➤ Review your marketing plan. You should have stated objectives and goals in the plan for both offline and online efforts, so that you make sure that what you do in real life properly reflects your brand.

89. What Sections Do I Include?

Importance

A social media strategy should, at minimum, contain enough information to fully address the expected goals and return on investment in social media efforts. Include the following sections:

✦ **Executive Summary**—This section includes a summary of the decisions made that led to the brand's use of social media. Content included in this summary could be a listing of the key team members, budget, and reasons for wanting to be on social media networks.

✦ **Benchmarks and Metrics**—Before deciding what networks to be a part of, it is important to first determine what success looks like for your brand. In this section, figure out what numbers you want to track, when you want to reach those numbers by, and what other factors may either affect or be affected by social media participation.

✦ **Communication Platforms**—The social media platforms you intend on participating in will be included in this section. Be sure to include not just the name of the platform, but also a description of what the platform is and how to use it. By doing so, you ensure that everyone participating understands the same intent and that if anybody new joins the effort, they'll be able to be easily brought up to speed. Also, individual platform benchmarks and metrics for each platform should be itemized since each network has varying availability for statistics and may be measured differently.

✦ **Key Influencers**—The key influencers for your network are the people who may be your brand's best evangelists.

✦ **Next Steps**—Including a list of the next steps or a calendar of action items is a highly recommended piece of the social media strategy.

> These sections are meant to describe only the minimum of what should be included in a strategy. Don't be afraid to include more detail. A strategy can't ever be too long!

Related Questions

➧ 4. How do I develop my brand strategy? **Page 13**

➧ 5. What is my brand's objective? **Page 18**

➧ 91. How do I figure out who my key influencers are? **Page 248**

➧ 97. How can I build influence? **Page 258**

Action Item

➧ Start writing your social media strategy. It doesn't have to be long—maybe even just a few pages. You can always develop and fine-tune it as you learn more about what you want to come out of your social media efforts.

90. What Are Key Influencers?

Importance

In general, people who use social media want to be able to control the conversation that surrounds their industry or individual brand. Finding the people online that can best support these efforts is the process of determining of whom your brand's key influencers consist. Key influencers do not have to be just people with large numbers of followers or friends, nor do they have to be thought leaders in your particular industry. They should simply be people or other brands that can help influence the people you target to be aware of and appreciate your brand.

Key influencers also don't have to just be people online. If your business is a retail shop, for example, you might want to look past just the people who can promote your business through the normal social media channels. Consider talking to local apartment building managers or businesses and hotels to build relationships with their staff or clientele. Then, using social media tools such as geo-location applications or QR codes, you can maximize relationships with people who might be strong influencers for your brand offline by using online practices.

 Related Question

➤ 6. Who is my target audience? **Page 20**

Action Item

➤ Make a list of those you think will be influencers for your brand. Base the list on who you know supports you and has a solid network.

Importance

91. How Do I Figure Out Who My Key Influencers Are?

To figure out who your key influencers are, take a look at who you believe could be evangelists for your brand. These people can be found in several different ways.

Perhaps they are people who converse with you, and engage with your brand often. Do you have people who continually reach out to you via one of your social networks and comment positively about your brand or services?

Maybe your key influencers are people who check in to your brand frequently on a geo-location service. Check out who your mayor on Foursquare is, but also check Foursquare to see who else is checking in frequently.

Your key influencers may even be offline, just starting to develop their online presence. This may be a time to help them align their online goals with yours.

 Related Questions

➜ 6. Who is my target audience? **Page 20**

➜ 7. Am I reflecting my brand? **Page 22**

➜ 76. Do I still need a business card? **Page 214**

Action Item

➜ If you have a Foursquare location set up, log into **Foursquare.com** and claim your venue. Then, look at the check-in history and cross-reference people who have checked in with Klout's influence scoring system. Doing research on people who already support your business will help you to have a better understanding of your support foundation.

92. How Should I Describe the Platforms I Choose?

Importance

Even if you fully understand each of the different platforms in which you choose to have your brand participate, it's best to include as much detail as possible in the descriptions. Descriptions should include a brief (or detailed, if you prefer) history of the service, how it is used, and the type of users that typically frequent the site. Equally as important is a description of how your brand intends to use the platform. If the intention is to use the service to listen to the conversation only, while another service is intended to be used as a public relations tool, this should be detailed in the platform description. That way, the intent or purpose cannot be misconstrued.

If you have a hard time determining how to describe a service or platform, check out that service's About page. It will likely have a detailed description of how the service came about, and how users can take advantage of its offering.

If you pull text or descriptions from a service site, be sure to reference that source. If you don't do so and people reference the strategy in other documents, it might be considered plagiarism.

 Related Questions

➤ 12. What social networks best fit my goals? **Page 40**

➤ 14. Why do I need to be selective? **Page 56**

Action Item

➤ Start off your platform descriptions with a statement from each respective site about its intended purpose. Then go into detail about how you intend to use that platform.

Importance

93. What Metrics Should I Use to Gauge My Return on Investment?

Different sites offer different metrics. The most common metrics are:

- Followers
- Fans
- Friends
- Backlinks
- Sales
- Referrals
- Social press coverage
- Geo-location check-ins
- Extended network
- Speed of growth
- Influence of followers/friends
- Engagement
- Page ranking
- SEO results

Many different tools are mentioned in Chapter 11, but you have to determine the reason why you want to know certain metrics before you decide to just go ahead and track them. Some measurements may mean a lot to your business, whereas others won't matter at all. Just like being selective about the services on which you create a brand presence, you should also narrow down the benchmarks and goals for your overall strategy.

The type of business you have will greatly determine the basic foundation of metrics you should track. Retail stores or businesses that depend on foot traffic will heavily rely on information about geo-location check-ins, whereas companies that don't take walk-in business (such as corporate headquarters) won't find much value in the information at all (other than which employees checks in the most).

A local brick-and-mortar also won't have as much need to have a high follower count, while an online magazine blog such as Mashable or HollywoodHotMoms.com might rely on follower and friend counts to help drive readership.

 Related Questions

➤ 14. Why do I need to be selective ? **Page 56**

➤ 73. How do I track what is said about my brand? **Page 202**

➤ 74. What brand monitoring tools can I use? **Page 204**

Action Items

➤ Set your benchmarks, then determine which metrics are most important to ensure positive ROI for your business.

➤ Create your spreadsheet to keep track of your growth.

Importance

94. What Do I Include as My Next Steps?

Writing a strategy is the first step, but implementation is the next. Detailing the action items is the plan for implementation and gives you specific, written deadlines for completion so that you can ensure your team stays on target.

This list of deadlines can also act as your editorial calendar for blog content or social network content. Although it lists overall action items, it does help to have a plan for the content you place on the sites on a regular basis.

During the strategy development session, specify a review period. This can be a week, a few weeks, a month, or even several months. The length of time you set aside as your "trial period" shouldn't be long, but it should feel like enough time for you and your team to feel like they had an opportunity to implement the strategy before they have to review feedback and results. A good standard of time to consider is 30 days, because the first two weeks will be mostly spent on setup, and another two weeks should have garnered enough reactions (or enough of a lack of reaction) for you and your team to look at the strategy and revise as necessary to improve the return on investment. Much longer than 30 days might result in too much time investment in the project right away, and it might take longer to recover from any negatively impacting issues. During this "trial period," you might also find that the goals you initially set for your brand were not actually goals you wanted to have. This discovery process will help you to realize that early on.

Once you've reached a point where you can review, go through every single step of the strategy and see where it can be improved based on the engagement or lack of engagement you've now been able to witness. If you're seeing your statistics grow, then consider ways to build on the foundation you've established. If you're seeing little or diminished results, the review period is the time to revise the strategy.

Related Questions

Action Item

➡ Create your editorial calendar!

Importance

95. How Often Should I Update My Strategy?

Success can be defined in so many ways. Be sure that your team is aware of what success means to the brand, and write it down. Because there are many different platforms, and there is the potential of millions of eyes on your brand, you will want to be certain that you have a solid understanding of the path you want your brand to follow online.

It can be easy in any situation to lose track of a goal and get distracted by everything going on around you. If you initially set out to reflect your expertise as a fitness instructor, but then find yourself starting an interactive public relations company, you might not have followed the path to your defined success. Although things may ultimately work to your benefit, allowing yourself to be derailed by external influences does not always work out. Even if you are okay with following a new path, be sure you revise your strategy to include this information.

Strategies should be considered working documents. As you begin to develop an online presence, you'll find that some things really don't go as planned. Perhaps you found a better or more efficient way to achieve your goals. Maybe a new service is available that you want to include in your plans. Either way, you'll need to be sure that your strategy is frequently updated to include every, and any, part of your plan and implementation.

 Related Questions

➡ 6. Who is my target audience? **Page 20**

➡ 7. Am I reflecting my brand? **Page 22**

➡ 76. Do I still need a business card? **Page 214**

➡ 79. What is a "Tweet-up?" **Page 220**

Action Item

➡ Schedule a date within one month to review your social media strategy and progress.

96. With Whom Should I Share My Strategy?

Importance

Share your strategy with everyone you can possibly share it with. Well, at least, share it with everyone who takes part in the implementation of your strategy and holds a stake in its efforts and goals. Ideally, everyone in the company would see the strategy or a portion of it. If you aren't comfortable with sharing the entire strategy with the company, consider at least developing a "policies and procedures" document to share so that you can be sure that they understand what is considered okay to do online and what is not okay.

Related Questions

- 4. How do I develop my brand strategy? **Page 13**
- 73. How do I track what is said about my brand? **Page 202**
- 74. What brand monitoring tools can I use? **Page 204**
- 77. Why does what I do in the real world matter? **Page 216**

Action Item

- Make a copy of your strategy for anyone with a public-facing role in the company.

Evolving a Brand

In this chapter:

- **97. How can I build influence?**
- **98. How can I keep my social media efforts interesting?**
- **99. How do I keep from being overwhelmed?**
- **100. Where do I go from here?**

?

Importance

97. How Can I Build Influence?

After you establish your social media strategy and identify your goals, you can begin your quest to build influence.

When trying to build influence, it's important to remember that numbers don't necessarily matter. A high number of followers for an account doesn't mean that those followers are high quality. Metrics for influence consider the quality of engagement from your followers instead.

So how do you engage your followers? Using monitoring tools like Klout (see Figure 15-1), as referenced in Chapter 11, you can gauge what your followers want to hear from you. When you use different types of content, you should use the monitoring tools to review the reactions to see how you can make improvements.

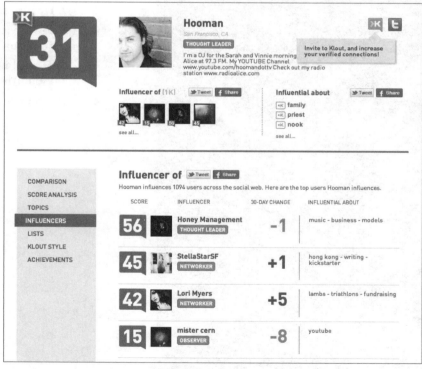

FIGURE 15-1: Services such as Klout can help you make sure you're on the right track to growing your influence.

Remember that the best content is content that includes some reason for others to respond. Whether the content is a question, an amazing photo, or some other call to action, each of these should reach out to the audience and have an appeal for a response based on a personal connection.

Regardless of whether your brand's purpose in developing a social media campaign has to do with wanting to become a thought leader in your industry, providing great customer service, or just joining the conversation, an inevitable result from going online is that your brand can become a part of a community. You can choose to have your brand be a leader or a follower, but either way, you will find your brand engaging with others in a public way. To have any influence in the social web, your brand must engage in public communication to have a chance for positive return on investment (ROI) on your campaign.

Although there are no specific guidelines regarding tweets, content should be relevant to your brand and to the image you want to portray. Tweets should also have a balance of announcement and engagement. Because Twitter is truly a conversational tool, best practices show that ensuring your stream flows two ways helps build your brand.

Some content ideas that may help your brand develop that conversation include the following:

- New blog posts
- Announcements
- Events
- Replies
- Direct messages
- Contests
- Personal thoughts and reflections that suit your brand
- Links to useful information or press
- Notes of appreciation to others who retweet your information or recommend you to others

As you develop your content and your experience grows, you will find that your style will naturally evolve. As it does, your comfort level with producing content should increase, and you'll be in a better position to assert yourself as an industry leader or "go-to resource" for information. Building influence is not something that is going to happen overnight, because it needs a foundation upon which to grow in order for it to prove valuable to your overall efforts.

Taking advantage of the resources and trying out the processes described in this book will help you to get started in your social media efforts, and you can use that foundation to develop your knowledge and grow your influence. You'll be able to measure your influence growth using the tools mentioned in Chapter 11 to help make sure you're headed in the right direction.

 Rule of Thumb   Spend some time "listening" before you jump into the conversation. Understanding what your audience wants to hear and see from your brand is key to creating and executing a strategy with positive ROI.

Related Questions

➤ 1. Why do I need a personal brand? **Page 2**

➤ 4. How do I develop my brand strategy? **Page 13**

➤ 10. How do I brand my online identity? **Page 34**

➤ 77. Why does what I do in the real world matter? **Page 216**

Action Item

➤ Compare three months of social media reports for your brand. Is there growth or a decline? See what factors might have caused your increase, or decrease, in overall influence and engagement. If you started veering off your social media plan course, you need to get back on track. If you stayed in line with your plans, it may be time to make some adjustments.

98. How Can I Keep My Social Media Efforts Interesting?

Importance

No strategy is ever 100% final. Understanding that conversations people have with brands and the ways brands interact with consumers are changing can help your brand take a look at what is going on in the social sites and adapt to the various changes as needed. Because these conversations are essentially happening in real time, you need to remember that engaging with others online is just like having a conversation in real life. Change truly is a constant, and learning how to roll with the changes is what can help to keep the efforts interesting.

Social media efforts can grow stale for various reasons. Users can simply find your updates to be less interesting and start engaging with you less. If your campaign started with contests, you may find it costly to keep up with the financial obligations for these promotions.

Having a conversation with someone using social media is no different than having a conversation in real life. Nobody wants to hear you talk all the time and sometimes you have to think of new things to talk about because you're not getting much feedback or interest from the other party. The great thing about social media is that you can look at numbers and statistics and quantify your efforts so that you can make a guided decision on how to proceed.

Use your statistics to review the areas that it appears your brand lacks. Use the RSS feeds or content aggregators to help find new content. Look to current events or pop culture to supplement the typical industry information you partake in. All these things should help you with your campaign and can help continue to assist with continually feeding you content.

Even big brands change their strategies or mix things up every once in a while. Sony Electronics is an example of a big brand that has different types of content on their social networks. It doesn't have just one way of communicating with its followers, and it finds ways to change the conversation to keep the conversation interesting (see Figure 15-2).

FIGURE 15-2: Sony knows how to keep the conversation interesting.

 Related Questions

→ 5. What is my brand's objective? **Page 18**

→ 7. Am I reflecting my brand? **Page 22**

→ 64. What sites can help me find relevant news? **Page 176**

→ 93. What metrics should I use to gauge my return on investment?
Page 250

Action Item

→ Use Twitter Search and look up current trending topics. If
possible, try to take part in these trending topics in a way
that puts your brand in a positive light.

99. How Do I Keep from Being Overwhelmed?

Importance

Participating in social media can take a lot of time. There are hundreds of millions of people using it, and just as much content being passed around. It's easy to start feeling overwhelmed. So what do you do?

Following are steps that you can take to keep from being overwhelmed.

1. **Make a schedule.** Similar to an editorial calendar, develop a schedule that can help you keep track of your content. Start by keeping track of your brand's key dates such as product or service releases. Then, taking the different types of content, schedule your topics in a manner that allows you to post during times that are important to your audience.

2. **It's all about the tools!** So many companies were founded on the idea that they could make the social media experience better. Third-party media companies such as Hootsuite, Seesmic, and UberMedia all have products that are supposed to make participation easier and more efficient. Most of these tools have scheduling features that enable you to post content without having to be tied to the computer.

3. **Take advantage of lists.** Twitter and Facebook both enable you to create lists for filtered content. Use these lists to help you more efficiently review content based on what you are interested in at the time.

4. **Learn to turn it off.** As you start to become involved in social media sites, you may find yourself drawn to participating all the time. Fight the urge to look at your Twitter feed first thing in the morning or to check your Facebook account before you go to bed. If you immerse yourself in social media right away, you might burn out fairly quickly. As with other things in life, too much of something is not always a good thing. Pace yourself so that you can endure.

Related Questions

➧ 5. What is my brand's objective? **Page 18**

➧ 14. Why do I need to be selective? **Page 56**

➧ 74. What brand monitoring tools can I use? **Page 204**

➧ 75. How can social media websites make this easier? **Page 212**

Action Item

➧ Install some social media applications on your phone and set them to send you alerts when you are mentioned or discussed on that site. Check to see if your mobile application has an option to turn off alerts during certain hours so that you don't get interrupted during your off time.

100. Where Do I Go from Here?

Importance

Now that you've asked all your questions, what do you do? It's time to start implementing what you've learned!

You know what social media is and how you can include it in your marketing efforts. Now take the strategy you wrote in Chapter 14 and start putting it into action.

So many people just dive into social media without really knowing what they're doing or understanding what they want to come out of their efforts, and this rarely results in positive ROI. More often, these people get quickly burned out or jaded by a lack of return. If you're planning to take part in social media for business or brand-building purposes, then you should approach social media as you would any other part of your business.

It's important to remember that social media is not meant to replace marketing; instead, it is another avenue to conduct marketing efforts. That's why the social media strategy needs to be included with the overall marketing plan and why you shouldn't create a social media strategy without first consulting with the overall objectives of your company.

 Related Questions

→ 4. How do I develop my brand strategy? **Page 13**

→ 13. How do I choose which sites to use? **Page 52**

→ 74. What brand monitoring tools can I use? **Page 204**

→ 77. Why does what I do in the real world matter? **Page 216**

Action Item

→ Get started! Implement your social media strategy. As you gain more experience and learn more about what you want to result from your efforts in social media, fine-tune your strategy as needed.

Index

I

ICQ, 42

ignoring inappropriate comments, 228–229

IM (instant messaging), 42, 48, 49

Import/Export tab, Google Reader, 89

inappropriate comments, 228–231, 240–241. *See also* spam

Incredibooth, 187

influence
  building, 258–260
  key, on brands, 245, 247–248
  Klout user influence styles, 120–123

informal market analysis, 20–21

informative blog style, 86–87

inspiration, blog posting and, 83–85, 93–94

Instagram, 187

instant messaging (IM), 42, 48, 49

interacting, on websites/blogs, 109

Interactions, Facebook analytics, 147

interesting content, 139–140

interesting conversations, 261–262

Internet Explorer, 195

Internet forums. *See* forums

Internet Relay Chat (IRC), 42–43

iPad applications, 178–179

Iran election fraud, 113–114

IRC (Internet Relay Chat), 42–43

J

JetBlue, 10–11, 24

Joomla, 75

Jooners, 222

juice, Google, 105, 106, 107

K

Karim, Jawed, 183

key influencers, 245, 247–248

keyword-focused title tag, 191

keywords, 193–194

Klout, 120–123, 207, 248, 258

Kutcher, Ashton, 50

L

Laipply, Judson, 183

Landor, Walter, 4

Langford, John, 98

language
  natural, 191
  obscenity, 27
  profanity, 44, 228, 231
  vulgar, 228, 231

Like button, 75, 143, 144, 150

likes. *See* Facebook

links (hyperlinks)
  backlinks, 103, 190, 197, 250
  building, 197–198
  deep, 192
  defined, 83
  embedded, 83
  link-baiting, 84
  nofollow, 234
  to profiles, 51, 118
  SEO and, 190, 191, 192